The Self-Love Affair

A Woman's Guide to a Daring & Mighty Life

Katie Phillips

Disclaimer: Although the author has made every effort to ensure that the information in this book was correct at press time, the author does not assume and hereby disclaims any liability to any party for any loss, damage, or disruption caused by errors or omissions, whether such errors or omissions result from negligence, accident, or any other cause.

This book is not intended as a substitute for the medical advice of physicians. The reader should regularly consult a physician in matters relating to his/her health and particularly with respect to any symptoms that may require diagnosis or medical attention.

First printing: 2015.
ISBN-13: 978-1514274682
ISBN-10: 151427468X

British Cataloguing Publication Data
A catalogue record of this book is available from
The British Library.

Also available on Kindle

FAR BETTER IT IS TO
DARE MIGHTY
THINGS to win glorious
triumphs
EVEN THOUGH CHECKERED BY FAILURE
than to take rank with those
TIMID SPIRITS
who neither enjoy
much NOR SUFFER
MUCH BECAUSE THEY LIVE IN THE
GREY TWILIGHT
that knows not
VICTORY
NOR defeat.

THEODORE ROOSEVELT

Contents

Awareness is the first step towards making change in your life so it is imperative to start our work with a massive life assessment and reality check.

We are moving away from the head, into the heart and connecting all parts of ourselves. This is where healing takes place and we are supported by our Spirit.

PART 3: MY VISION. MY FUTURE.   167

You are a creator. It's time to dream big and manifest your deepest desires in a way that is an authentic reflection of you!

GRATITUDE

The content of this book is the culmination of several years committed to my personal and spiritual development. The material I share with you is a kaleidoscopic collage of teachings which I have absorbed from numerous mentors, coaches, authors, teachers, psychologists, colleagues, friends and family. Sadly, I am unable to pinpoint every single person and credit them individually. I wish I could. Without the guidance, inspiration and knowledge I have gained from others, my life wouldn't be what it is today and my gratitude is enormous.

That said, I desire to give my heartfelt thanks to Mum and Dad.

Marion and Bernard.

Just typing those two names brings tears to my eyes.

I love you both and I am so grateful for every single lesson you have taught me.

INTRODUCTION

D&M

Adjective

1. the Australian abbreviation for Deep and Meaningful. Usually used to describe the essence of a conversation. *We had a D&M.*

2. the universal abbreviation for Daring and Mighty. Usually used to describe how an individual knows, loves and creates him or herself. Used to describe a code of living. *She is so daring and mighty!*

A Quick D&M

As little as three years ago, my predominant feelings were of sadness, depression, worry, fear, guilt, overwhelm and crippling anxiety. My sense of self was miniscule. Any sense of worthiness came from the outside – my career, my relationship, my 'achievements'. I felt disconnected – to myself and the world around me. It was like having a permanent out of body experience. Sometimes I watched myself in conversation with others as if I wasn't present. I was completely detached from the experience and the awareness of that was terrifying. I awoke every morning in panic, with the weight of anxiety so heavy in my chest that my breathing could barely keep up with my pounding heart. That is how I started the day! My emotions had a life of their own. I was their victim. It was my 'lot' in life to feel lost and empty. At the core of me was a black hole – a void to be filled – and I had no idea how to heal it. So I unconsciously numbed it with addictions to romantic relationships, drama, alcohol, caffeine and television.

What most people saw was a smiley, intelligent, confident, attractive woman who lived a fun and adventurous life. She travelled the world, had an exciting career and was never short of boyfriends and good times. She was a story teller – her escapades, the men, the drama, the 'living' was witty and, being Australian, beautifully self-deprecating.

The distance between the truth of how I felt and what I projected to the world was mammoth. The scary thing is that I didn't even know I was doing it. I didn't know any other way. The way I felt, the ways I behaved, what I allowed others to see, what I even allowed myself to see was unconscious and habitual. I had convinced myself I was 'happy' because on the outside, things looked pretty good and I lived a far from 'ordinary' life. Surely this was as good as it got? In my gut though, I knew there was a chance that wasn't really the case. A little voice that suggested perhaps I could feel better on the inside. That I didn't have to feel damaged and empty.

A decade ago I started grief therapy to help me come to terms with my mother's suicide some years earlier and it was only then that I started to witness this gap between what I showed the world and what I truly felt. I discovered an awareness of my feelings because I started to open up to the possibility that I could feel a different way. That had never occurred to me! I had felt anxious and worried since I was a little girl. I didn't know anything else. Awakening to the concept that there could be another way was terrifying at first because it was the unknown. But, as present as that black hole was, I always had an awareness of a light inside me that was special in some way. I knew deep down that I was precious and unique and loveable. I just didn't know how to hold onto those thoughts. To believe them.

And so my journey began. I started to realise that my life could be anything I wanted it to be. More importantly, that I could feel any way I wanted to feel. That happiness was actually in my control. That life isn't about survival. It's about creation. I no longer wanted to sleep walk through my life. I wanted to be awake. Even if that meant having to face up to some deeply painful stuff. I knew it was the only way forward. I decided that I wanted my life to be an authentic reflection of me. I realised that was the point of everything!

The decision to embark on creating a life that makes me feel happy, connected, peaceful and authentic was profound. That was 10 years ago. The majority of the last decade has been incredibly painful. I had 30 years of unconscious living, deeply ingrained negative belief systems and behavioural patterns to overcome. In fact, developing an awareness of the tough feelings meant they worsened before they improved! But the rewards have been so so worth it. To feel free, able to celebrate my vulnerability and live the truth of my heart from a place of deep self-knowing and self-love is priceless. And this is what I want for others. I know it is possible and I am now in a place that enables me to share my experience and truly be of service. It has become my purpose.

Gimme The Low Down

Righto, let's get down to business. Before you read much further, let's work out if this book is for you because I do not want to waste your time. Life is precious!

If my story resonated with you and you found yourself saying, 'Yes! I want to feel like that too!' then it is likely you will get lots of good stuff out of this book. And I am so excited for you!

To be clear, this book is only for people willing to do the work. Let me say that again: you need to DO THE WORK. If you want a nice, soft, touchy feely book, this is not the read for you. This book will open you up and you are likely to get in touch with some pretty painful stuff. Please know, however, that you will be rewarded for your efforts and I will support you all the way.

If you are fed up with feeling the way you do and have even the tiniest gut feeling that it could be possible to feel better, then this book is for you.

If you are feeling stuck and are ready to roll up your sleeves and get to the bottom of why you feel that way, then this book is for you.

If you are ready to believe that it is possible to survive leaving your comfort zone for something better, then this book is for you.

If you are willing to open your mind to all that I suggest, even the seemingly 'out there', 'woo waa', 'hippy shit' concepts, then this book is for you.

If you are prepared to dedicate time to doing the exercises I suggest, then this book is for you.

If you can deal with being told some cold hard truths because you trust I have your best interests at heart, then this book is for you.

If you are ready to stop the thinking that goes, *"When I have X I will be happy,"* or *"If I could Y I would be happy,"* then this book is for you.

If you are willing to stop waiting for a 'quick fix' to magically arrive on your doorstep, then this book is for you.

If you really want to know who you are, then this book is for you.

If you are ready to create a life that you love, then this book is for you.

If you are prepared to believe that I have 'been there, done that', that I 'walk my talk' and that I truly care about your journey, then this book is for you.

If you are prepared to accept that I do not have all the answers and am dedicated to helping you with all that I know, in the ways that I know best based on what worked for me, then this book is for you.

If you desire to be Daring and Mighty, then this book is most definitely for you!

Yes?

Ooh, I think I just heard you jump on board! Strap yourself in, this is gonna be one mighty ride!

Before we get going I want to recognise that, as exciting as this journey will be, I know you are very likely feeling a little nervous. It's a bit like getting onto a rollercoaster. You line up for ages, full of anticipation, watching the faces of the other joy riders - a mixture of terror and pure joy and, as they disembark, a mixture of excited delight and green nausea! By the time you hop into your carriage and strap yourself in, you are practically feverish. You know it's going to be exhilarating but it's going to scare the pants off you too! By the end though, despite feeling a little jaded, you are fired up and looking for your next adrenaline rush!

This Daring & Mighty journey isn't dissimilar. It is totally human to be feeling excited and a little nervous right now. You know you are about to commit to something life-changing and that's a bit scary. So I bet you would like to hear something a little soft and fluffy about now? Something the rollercoaster operator wouldn't give you? (See, I have your back already!)

You deserve a *comfort cuddle.*

Close your eyes and imagine great big loving arms are wrapped about you, giving you a massive reassuring squeeze. Imagine all your fear and anxiety being absorbed by this cuddle. You feel like a tiny child and you have total faith that you are held safe. And breathe. It's all going to be ok!

Please let me reassure you that this book isn't all about pain and hard work. You will also experience pure joy, divine relaxation, deep connection, fabulous self-belief, a life vision and purpose, profound faith, awakened authenticity and, most of all, blissful self-love. Miraculous, life-changing love.

Are you ready to make a decision?

Yes?

Then it's time for your first exercise!

 *AN EXERCISE*

Get yourself something to write on. If you don't have a pretty journal just now, it doesn't matter. You can get one of those later. Right now, just grab a piece of paper and write about WHY you want to read this book and WHAT you desire to get out of it. Set your INTENTION right now, while you are really feeling it. The last couple of pages have moved you in some way, giving you the impetus to carry on reading and I don't want you to forget why you are making this decision. Say YES to discovering a way to feel better and to creating a life you love. The aim of this writing exercise is to start the process of getting honest with where you are at now and where you desire to be.

Have a think about what you specifically want to heal in your life. What are you fed up with? What simply has to change? Do you have a specific goal you want to achieve? There is a reason you picked up this book. What was that reason?

You know what is right for you. Write from your heart. It could be half a page, it could be several pages but do not cheat yourself – write everything that is in your heart. The more you write now, the more evidence you will have later of how far you have come. That evidence builds your faith and trust in the process you are about to embark on. It will show you how far you have come on days when you are considering giving up. It will remind you why you started the process in the first place. Never lose sight of your REASON WHY. That is the key to persistence.

Please do not type this. Something magical happens when we put pen to paper. Somehow our Spirit is able to freely speak through and we write our most powerful, heartfelt truths.

One day you will look back at this and give yourself a huge hug because you will witness how far you have come. Oh, did I mention that hugging yourself will probably become 'normal'....!?

When you feel you have written all you need, please write a promise to yourself. A vow that clearly defines the decision you are making. This promise needs to go somewhere that allows you to read it regularly. Perhaps on the fridge, stuck to your mirror; it could be the screensaver on your computer or smartphone. Whatever works for you. Your promise needs to be as simple as possible and it needs to emote a positive feeling in you. A feeling of excitement and optimism. Here are a few ideas:

"I promise to do everything in my power to create a life that I love. Because I deserve it!"

"I vow to overcome my fears and do all it takes to feel happy and complete!"

"I deserve to have a Daring & Mighty life and I am committed to a journey of change and growth!"

"I want my life to be an authentic reflection of who I truly am and I am committed to doing everything in my power to make that happen."

"I choose to feel connected and complete and I am committed to overcoming all that has been holding me back. I deserve to have a life I love."

"I want to know love. I will do anything it takes. This is my vow."

"I want to know who I am and become the best version of me! I am committed to this journey of discovery."

"I want to live the truth of my heart. I welcome the journey and will give it all I have! I promise."

Happy writing! It's time to give yourself permission to shine. I'll go get my sunnies.....! (Oh, that's Aussie for sunglasses!)

I am... *YOUR AFFIRMATION*

Your first affirmation is in the form of a song, affirming the promise you are about to write. Say it loud, sing it proud!

(Check out my Spotify Playlist to listen - http://spoti.fi/1H0Gvz0)

"Permission to Shine" - Bachelor Girl

I'm gonna give myself permission to shine

I'm gonna shine so bright

Gonna make every head wanna turn

You're finally gonna see me

Give myself permission to shine

Gonna light up the night

Shine a little of my light on the world

What's The Upshot?

You are Daring & Mighty!

Yep! By making the commitment above, you have just joined a tribe of people who are doggedly determined to create a life that is an awesome reflection of the magnificent beauty that's inside. Their internal reality matches their external reality. And these people know that keeping that balance is a life-long commitment. They also know it becomes the most natural and wonderful and obvious way of living.

So, welcome!

Commitment to the Daring & Mighty code of living has many, many benefits. It is seriously cool. Makes you wonder why only the select few sign up. I mean, check these out:

- You love yourself!

- You will make a profound difference in the world!

- You are part of a bright and beautiful tribe!

- You get to live within your own values!

- You experience deep connection to yourself and with others!

- You get to really, truly know yourself!

- You are awake and living consciously!

- You feel deeply that you are living into your destiny!

- You know the feeling of true forgiveness!

- You are present and living in the now!

- You serve your own vision – not someone else's!

- You feel excited for your life because you discover what you are meant to do!

- You feel ever-growing gratitude for all you have!

- You have deep, authentic, supportive, loving friendships!

- You are connected with your own Spirit and your higher power!

- You have ever-growing faith that you are held safe by the Universe!

- You have tools that will keep your internal and external worlds in balance!

- You know how to bring yourself back to a calm, peaceful place whenever you need to!

- You have discovered how powerful you are and have developed self-mastery!

Quite frankly, being Daring & Mighty means you are a Super Hero! Yep! But a really cool one. No big red granny pants for you. And you don't hide behind a mask. No, you are SuperStylin' and know how to rock your swagger. Hell yeah!

You are a unique individual. You know, not many people stop long enough to ask themselves what they really want from their life. They just let life happen to them. Remember that fabulous John Lennon quote:

"Life is what happens to you when you are busy making other plans."

Not you! Nope. You have taken the bull by the horns and are now the head honcho of your own rodeo. Yeehaa!

Most people are not even aware, let alone have the belief, that they can create their own happiness either. You are different. You dare to believe it is possible. You're a step ahead, baby!

Do you have supersonic vision too?

I was being facetious but actually, yes, you do! You have mighty vision because you already see that your world can look different. You are preparing to access and harness the creative power inside you to turn your visions into supersonic reality.

And, like all Super Heroes, you have a motivational back-story. Your story, the stuff that you are fed up with and determined to change - that stuff's pure gold, baby! That's the stuff that will propel you forward. You have decided that you want more from your life. You have a *motivation*. You are turning things on their head. Like a magnet, where there's a negative there is always a positive. My friend, you are going to magnetise the most amazing new stuff to replace the old.

Ah! You are gonna fly. Well clearly - that's what Super Heroes do. I am so excited for you!

What Now?

Well, now that you have discovered the awesome truth that you are in fact a Super Hero, before we look at exactly how this book will work and what you can expect to be doing, we need to tackle the only thing that could get in your way.

What? Surely nothing could stop the superhuman strength and determination of a super crusader? Well, actually yes. The most terrifying nemesis of all. Fear. (Da da daaaaaaa!)

Fear could stop you from reading even the next paragraph so I want to tackle that immediately and give you a fighting chance of finishing this book. I want to tell you what fear really is and encourage you to laugh in the face of it. It's time to get serious for a minute.

"I learned that courage was not the absence of fear, but the triumph over it. The brave man is not he who does not feel afraid, but he who conquers that fear." Nelson Mandela

Mr. Mandela has got it in one. He isn't ignoring the existence of fear. It is very real and incredibly destructive. It is what stops you from claiming pretty much anything you want to be, do or have. In fact, fear can be so strong that you do not even allow yourself to dream that things could be different. It isn't even an option. Sadly, the majority of people allow fear to run their lives like this. Even scarier, they don't even realise they're doing it because it hides out in your subconscious. That's the power of fear. It's a sneaky little sucker!

My Mac dictionary says fear is an 'unpleasant emotion'. That is the understatement of the century! Fear can paralyze you. Then it will physically grip your throat and choke the life out of you. But, as 'real' as it feels, the shocking truth is that fear is just a story! Fear is **F**alse **E**vidence **A**ppearing **R**eal. Perhaps you have heard that acronym before?

Fear is the powerful voice of your subconscious and your subconscious is all parts of you at all ages. It is the four-year-old, 14-year-old, 24-year-old and you today - all blended into one. It will usually have the reasoned authority of the adult you today blended with, say, the emotional charge of the two-year-old you. The adult voice may not even be yours - it could be the voice of a parent or teacher - just as long as it gets your attention! Your subconscious is the sum of every life experience, every lesson, every belief, every other voice you have ever adopted as defining who you are. (By the way, you didn't have a choice in many of the beliefs you have taken on as yours - but we will come to that later).

As an adult, you now have a choice whether or not to listen to the stories of your subconscious. With awareness comes choice. You know the drill!

"Nothing in life is to be feared, it is only to be understood. Now is the time to understand more, so that we may fear less." Marie Curie

If you choose to listen to the voice of fear, you make the story real. We only give fear power over us if we choose to listen to it. So, if we have a choice, why do we listen to these stories? Excellent question! Because the voice of fear is intellectual and highly emotionally charged. It is a cleverly convincing and authoritative voice which seemingly comes from your intellectual, reasoned mind. Clinging to the hand of this adult voice are the emotional extremes of a small child - throwing tantrums one minute, craving cuddles and approval the next. As soon as you add an emotional charge to an idea, it is given huge power.

Our fear-based stories are largely founded on false belief systems we mostly inherited when we were very young. We will look more closely at limiting beliefs and how we learn them shortly. For now, all I want you to consider is the truth that your fear is a story. There are usually two sides to every story, right? So, for now, please stay open to the idea that the stories you are telling yourself - the ones that make you feel scared and stuck - are NOT TRUE.

Deciding to improve your life might seem like a great idea. And it is. However, that will require you to change. Believe it or not, if where you are at is all that you know, then that has become your *comfort* zone. Let's think of your comfort zone as a little nest where you have been living, warm and cozy, for a long, long time. No matter how uncomfortable and fed up you are, all you know is this nest, with all its muck and junk and old baggage. It's actually pretty dirty and full of stuff you no longer need. And yet it is your safe haven. For some reason, us humans are not too keen to move into a new nest without knowing exactly what it looks and feels like. If that nest doesn't exist yet, how can we trust that it will be better than where we are? Do we even want 'better' when what we have now is fine? I mean, better might mean we need to step up a gear in some way and because we don't know what *that* will look like, it's a double whammy and we find ourselves more determined than ever to stay put in our 'fine' nest. You know what the acronym for "FINE" is, don't you? **F**ucked up, **I**nsecure, **N**eurotic and **E**motional. Gosh, why on earth do we want to live with that? That's the power of fear. And we tend to fear success even more than failure! Go figure.

"Always remember the acronym for "FEAR" can mean one of two things: Fuck Everything And Run or Face Everything And Recover." Cupcake Brown

Even if your comfort zone is uncomfortable, it can motivate you to either stay put or run a mile because fear of the unknown can appear to be even more uncomfortable. That's why so many people sleep walk through their lives. They would rather stay unconscious and 'comfortable' than conscious, in connection with the voice of their truth, and therefore risk having to CHANGE. How many people do you know stay in a job they don't like because of fear? They are terrified that if they leave the job that is making them unhappy they may not ever get a better job, they will never earn enough money if they follow their heart, perhaps they are not clever or capable enough to do anything else. Who *are* they without the job? And so it goes on! Fear is a powerful tool to keep you 'safe'. Fear's job is to sabotage the voice of your Truth.

There is a huge difference between living in fear and being aware of fear. You have probably heard many times that awareness of something is the first step to conquering it? Same goes here. You, my friend, have made a decision to wake up. So your awareness around what you fear and why you fear it is going to grow. Please know that this is a positive thing.

When I *lived in fear* I was the 'victim' of anxiety, depression, worry and fatigue. My limiting beliefs totally ran the show and I was very stuck. It was absolutely exhausting! Choosing to recognise my fear began a journey of self-discovery that enabled me to untangle and understand the stories I was telling myself and why. That was the key to unlocking the paralysis and being truly free.

"Expose yourself to your deepest fear; after that, fear has no power, and the fear of freedom shrinks and vanishes. You are free." Jim Morrison

Most of my life, I have been terrified of just about everything. I was a truly anxious, worried little girl and fear was my buddy. When I picture myself at the age of four, I am horrified by what I see. I literally used to worry about how much I worried! I would often crawl into my mum's side of the bed at night and say, "Mummy, I have a worry." Yet I never knew what the worry was. I just felt unsafe - as if the ground beneath me could disappear at any moment. There were good reasons for this - a clinically depressed mum and an emotionally absent dad. They did their best and they loved me but they too were driven by fear. It consumed them for various reasons and it manifested itself in many different ways. Oh, how I wish they knew then what I have learned.

My biggest fear was losing my parents. As a young girl, although I didn't consciously know it or understand it, I always feared losing Mum to her depression and Dad to another woman. That underpinning fear evolved into many different manifestations of fear.

I grew up worrying that I wasn't perfect enough, pretty enough, clever enough, cool enough, sporty enough, sexy enough, happy enough. Then I worried I was too clever, too straight, too skinny, too damaged, too uptight, too cold, too shy, too promiscuous, too unloveable. Boy, it was exhausting! But I didn't know anything else. I didn't know I had a choice.

My worst fears came true. My dad had affairs and after a few false starts, eventually left. My mum took her own life. In my early twenties, with my deepest fears realised, my fear mutated into deep distrust of the authenticity, safety and reliability of any human relationship. Yep, a few biggies in there!!

All sounds pretty horrible, right? The thing is, I actually feel blessed. All of my experience has been the key to my freedom. To truly claim it and choose a life that is based on love. Not fear. I have overcome some absolutely enormous fear-based obstacles and it is an ongoing journey because being aware of fear does not mean that it will disappear. I may have managed to disappear some big fears, but there are always going to be others to deal with, depending on how far I am willing to move away from my comfort zone. Mandela was right on the money earlier when he said the brave man is the one who triumphs over his fear. Accepting fear as a reality of life is the first step to conquering it.

I experience fear every single day. In fact, the more I tread the Daring & Mighty path, the more fear I come up against. The more I get in touch with my truth and what I really want for my life, the bigger leaps of faith I take. So I *know* fear is going to come up. I have accepted it as normal. I have journeyed a long time and am pretty quick to notice when limiting beliefs are coming up to challenge me. I recognise them for what they are and I choose to push on, regardless. Sometimes I need some help to move forward so will call a friend or a coach to support me through it. My determination to conquer it pushes me onwards and I put two fingers up at fear. It feels great to triumph over it!

Now that we are getting clarity on what fear really is, I want to highlight the two biggest fears that pretty much encompass all varieties: fear of failure and fear of success. Would you believe that fear of success is what the majority of people suffer the most!? As you progress through this book that fact will become less shocking because you will start to witness how mighty powerful you are. Learning to harness that power is an *exciting* learning curve - how many times have you heard that fear and excitement are the same thing!?!

I love what Marianne Williamson says about our fear of success:

"Our deepest fear is not that we are inadequate. Our deepest fear is that we are powerful beyond measure. It is our light, not our darkness, that most frightens us. We ask ourselves, who am I to be brilliant, gorgeous, talented, fabulous? Actually, who are you not to be?"

I have wanted to write this book for a long time. I have been researching, making notes, putting myself through rigorous coaching and writing bits and bobs for around three years. When the day arrived that I felt clear on what my book was about and certain that I had the content sorted, I made the decision to start writing. Properly! I was genuinely excited to tell the world that I was writing a book, but do you know what thoughts hit me? Check these babies out:

- "I have no idea what I am talking about."

- "It's going to be so short, it will be a joke!"

- "Who the hell am I to tell other people how to improve their lives?"

- "What qualifications do I have to write a book like this?"

- "People are going to judge me and talk about what a ridiculous idea this is behind my back!"

- "What if people like the book and I am asked to speak at events? I am terrified of public speaking!"

- "What if the book is successful? My whole life will go under the spotlight! I am not strong enough for that."

- "If my business becomes really successful, I will lose my life balance and get overwhelmed."

Even though working towards the moment of sitting and actually writing the book for so long was a dream come true. Even though I deeply believed in the planned content. Even though I had mountains of evidence and am living proof that this process works. Even though I have actually become quite good at public speaking and running workshops. Even though I know that a successful business will actually give me the financial freedom to manage my life even better than I am now. Even though I quite like to be the centre of attention! Despite all that, my subconscious mind still kicked in and tried to sabotage it all. I was really, really horrible to myself. For a while I even listened. Even though I know better! Fear is a sneaky, sneaky little bastard! The fact that you are holding the book and reading it is a great big two fingers up to fear!

My example I will share around fear of failure relates to my business too.

My business, 'Daring & Mighty', was born of a range of affirmations I wrote and turned into designs for wall art. I wanted to inspire people and give them access to the power of affirmations in a creative, funky way. The motivation behind the development of this artwork was so simplistic and heartfelt and although I wanted to sell it, it never occurred to me that this was the beginning of a retail business venture. When I decided to turn my passion into a 'proper' business, my work stopped 'flowing' and fear hit the fan! Wow, suddenly my 'hobby' would be in the public domain, up for judgement and scrutiny. I was stepping away from my safe corporate world of event management into the 'woo waa' spiritual domain and, worse, therapy and personal development. Gulp!

- "You are crazy. People will think you have lost your mind!"

- "You will never make any money out of this. You have a child. You are a single parent. Don't be so bloody irresponsible!"

- "You can't make money out of art! You should keep it as a hobby."

- "You do not know how to sell. You do not know how to make money."

- "You have no idea how to run a business, let alone a retail business!"

- "Get real, Katie!"

- "Just think how embarrassed you will feel when this fails."

When I had my biggest wobble it was over choosing the colours for each design. I had to have a coaching session around it, I was so distraught! Suddenly, the passion and pure joy I found in colour became my worst nightmare. The colour selection had to be 'perfect'. I could not stuff it up. It felt like the biggest decision of my life. Wow, isn't it incredible how fear can distort the simplest things well out of proportion?! This experience really highlighted for me that fear is just a story. That all the nasty things I was telling myself, my need for perfection and approval were based on limiting beliefs that I had held since I was a small child. When I realised that fears of being imperfect were running the show, I was actually able to turn them on their head and the biggest selling point of my hand-made wooden wall art became the very fact that each piece of timber is imperfect and more beautiful as a result! And would you believe that when I got over myself and my need for the colours to be perfect, the Universe stepped in and showed me the full colour palette I was to use. I no longer had to figure it out. My coach had handed me a box of tissues during our 'colour therapy' session and the box was covered in colourful Matisse-style flowers. When the penny dropped and I saw the story I had been telling myself, I noticed the colours on the tissue box I had been crying into. I wish you could have seen my joy in that moment. When I listen to my truth - not the crappy stories of my subconscious - something miraculous happens. In that moment, it was as simple as a mix of colours on a tissue box.

The knowledge that my fears are just a story has been backed up by loads and loads of proof that something larger than me is holding me safe. No matter what choices I make, I am going to be ok. I know without doubt that this is the truth. Having faced some of my deepest, darkest, most terrifying fears, I have kind of developed a bolshy 'come on, show me what you've got!' attitude towards fear because I know that a loving Universe has my back.

The exact opposite of fear is love. Love is as equally present within you as fear but when love is running the show, fear doesn't stand a bloody chance! I can't wait to tell you more about this later in the book because learning to access the loving power within you and the loving power that is all around and holding you will be your key to freedom. Your key to a life that is not stuck in fear but one that is brimming with limitless possibilities. Best of all, you will love yourself!

John Lennon says it perfectly:

There are two basic motivating forces: fear and love. When we are afraid, we pull back from life. When we are in love, we open to all that life has to offer with passion, excitement, and acceptance. We need to learn to love ourselves first, in all our glory and our imperfections. If we cannot love ourselves, we cannot fully open to our ability to love others or our potential to create. Evolution and all hopes for a better world rest in the fearlessness and open-hearted vision of people who embrace life.

And let's hear it from Oprah!

I believe that every single event in life happens as an opportunity to choose love over fear. Oprah Winfrey

Now, let's laugh in the face of fear.

I tend to scare myself. Stephen King

Priceless!

 *AN EXERCISE*

I have a task for you that will help you start to witness your fear-based thoughts. I want you to start listening to what your subconscious mind is saying to you. Tune in to the conversations you have with yourself.

How are you talking to yourself? Notice the tone of the voice. Is it kind and supportive? Is it destructive and pessimistic?

How frequent is the chatter inside your head?

When you look in the mirror, what do you hear?

When you consider going to the gym, what do you say to yourself?

If you have been thinking about a job change, what stories are you telling yourself around that? When you are hanging out with your children, what is the dialogue in your head?

If you make a mistake, whose voice do you hear and what is it saying?

When someone prepares to take a photograph of you, what are you thinking?

When driving and someone cuts you off, what do you say to yourself?

Notice what experiences cause your internal chatter. What situations or experiences are you avoiding?

Consider who is speaking to you. Is it you? If it is, how old are you? Is it a teacher? A parent? A relative?

What are the feelings attached to the message? Do you feel angry? Sensitive? Defensive? Scared? Defeated? Excited? Sad?

How do you behave when you are having these fearful thoughts? Do you do anything to block them, or numb them out?

Please be kind to yourself when making notes on the above. I always ask my clients to do this exercise before we work together and the majority are quite shocked at what they discover. They knew they had a self-sabotaging voice but they hadn't realised just how loud and regular and mean it really was. Then they are tempted to add another nasty voice to their repertoire – something like, "Oh my God, I cannot believe you talk to yourself like that! That is so typical of you!" **Please don't be tempted to give yourself a hard time!** That is not the point of this exercise. I want you to start to learn the practice of being your own silent observer. I want you to witness yourself as if you are outside of yourself, with compassion, understanding and love. You are not to blame for the way you subconsciously speak to yourself. This is a brand new awareness and this exercise is going to help you enormously to understand where these beliefs have come from and what the truth really is.

Remember, awareness is the first step toward change! It is the first step towards being Daring & Mighty!

 *PUMP UP THE VOLUME*

"The Fear" - Ben Howard

I am... *YOUR AFFIRMATION*

My fearful thoughts are just a story. I observe them with compassion and kindness.

The First Day of the Rest of Your Life!

Ok, so now we need to get you prepared for the rest of this book. You are probably gagging to know what to expect! If you are like me, you like to get everything lined up and ready to go. (I have embraced my inner 'gold star student'! Better to acknowledge and accept her than tell myself I am a 'goody two shoes', right!) So here's the deal:

This book is now about to divide into three sections:

Part 1:   Right Here, Right Now

Part 2:   My Spirit, My Truth

Part 3:   My Vision. My Future.

As you may have already guessed, there are going to be a lot of writing exercises throughout this book. I find journalling an incredibly powerful tool because it gives an outlet to those thoughts that swirl round and round in your head. They need to be set free! Your pen and paper will liberate them.

Buy yourself a journal (there's a great website called www.daringandmighty.com that stocks gorgeous recycled leather journals....just an idea....!). Make your journal special -something that inspires you and that you can keep with you at all times. You never know when you will get the urge to write!

There are three more tools that we will use regularly. Meditation, Music and Affirmations.

Please start thinking about a space where you can meditate. Locate a quiet area in your home where you will not be disturbed (by kids, phones, computers, TV, stereo etc). If you have the room, create a special meditation zone and fill it with things that make you feel peaceful and relaxed such as candles, incense, fresh flowers, pictures or crystals. Make sure you have something comfortable and supportive to sit on, whether that be a chair or a meditation pillow. A blanket nearby is usually a good idea as you may get a little chilly. I don't have a specific room but I do have my great big pink Lazy Lady! I love her. She is an oversized beanbag. I set her up and put a pretty plate on the floor in front of me with candles and frankincense. Sometimes I just sit on my couch but there are always candles lit and something that smells great wafting about the room! Just the process of lighting the candles changes the energy of the space for me and signifies that my intention is to connect to the light within me and beyond me. We lack rituals in our western society and it's nice to add them where we can to give our actions and experiences a deeper meaning.

You can access a free download of all the meditations included in this book here: http://daringandmighty.com/meditation-library

Music is an incredibly powerful tool and one I use a lot because it adds fabulous emotive energy to experiences around change and growth. As you know, hearing a song that was once played at a special occasion will bring back all the memories and feelings of that moment. As we learn new things on this Daring & Mighty process, I will attach a song for you to listen to which I hope will enliven and energise the experience further for you. Then, whenever you hear that song, you can re-live and celebrate your new awareness or learning. I would like to encourage you to 'follow' my Spotify Playlist because all the songs I include here will be at your fingertips to play in the moment. (http://spoti.fi/1H0Gvz0). You may like to create your own Daring & Mighty playlist and add songs that work for you too. It will become a wonderful set of music to lift your spirits and help you to connect to the beautiful truth of you, way after finishing this book.

After every writing exercise or meditation, I will give you an affirmation. This is a sentence for you to repeat to yourself throughout the day to reinforce something that you have just learned or experienced. The affirmation may even be some song words. You might like to write the affirmation onto a slip of paper and pop it in your purse, so that every time you open it, you will be reminded of your thought for the day. Perhaps update your computer screensaver with the words. Or set an alarm on your phone to ping through the words every couple of hours. Whatever works for you. The words will mean you will stop what you are doing, even if only for a few seconds, and remember the truth of you and the importance of the journey you are on – because your connection to you is more important than anything else!

I would like to encourage you at this point to consider who will be in your Daring & Mighty Posse. Who will be there to share your stories and experiences? To offer you support on this journey? And vice versa? We discovered that you are in fact a Super Hero and working alone is part and parcel of that. Much of the work you do will be on your own because that is the only way forward. However, think of the Super Hero teams who are stronger because they have the power of many. Think Fantastic Four, The X-Men, The Avengers. I encourage you to mastermind with others reading this book. Perhaps you have friends reading it or if not, there is always my private Facebook Group – The Self-Love Hubb: https://www.facebook.com/groups/theselflovehubb – which is a wonderful community of like-minded crusaders. Share your stories, your successes, the stuff you are finding tough. Perhaps create your own Daring & Mighty Power Posse - get together and discuss the concepts in this book and your experiences. Everyone's story and experience will resonate with someone else. To share is to grow.

"The greatest good you can do for another is not just to share your riches but to reveal to him his own." Benjamin Disraeli

All the concepts in this book have been taught to me by others. There is nothing new here. The tools and techniques I am going to share with you have been proven to work time and time again. When I embarked on a mission to save my life (yes, that is how it felt!) 10 years ago, I decided to try everything. I was not going to stop until I found what worked for me and, as I have already confessed, I am a bit of an A+ student so everything I tried I committed to 100% and gave it my all. Grief Therapy, Cognitive Behavioural Therapy (CBT), Psychodynamic Counselling, Self-Help Books and Tapes, Dynamic Life Coaching, The Demartini Method, In Depth Values Analysis, Emotional Freedom Technique (EFT), Neuro Linguistic Programming (NLP), Hypnotherapy, Laws of Attraction & Manifesting, Vision Boarding, Meditation. You name it, I gave it a go. Every one of the above helped in their own way and naturally some methods were more powerful than others. It was when I discovered meditation that my world really started to change and I was led to doing the Hoffman Process – an eight-day residential self-development programme. I experienced a profound spiritual awakening while on the process and discovered a way to clear the last remaining, most stubborn blocks and limiting beliefs which were still holding me back.

What I share in this book is a blend of all I have learned. Authenticity is my highest value so it is important that you know I am not claiming all the processes in this book as my own and I will acknowledge my teachers and the originators of any unique theories or processes wherever appropriate.

My wish is that you get everything you need right now from this book. These pages have been written with you, the reader, in my heart and with love.

Please stay open-minded, allow yourself to go with the flow and allow this process to work its magic!

My hope is that you learn to tune into yourself in a loving way, allowing you to live your truth, shine your light on the world and, very simply, spread love.

Thank you for trusting me.

Be Daring. Be Mighty.

 *PUMP UP THE VOLUME!*

"Positively Somewhere" - Melanie C

"I Choose" - India Arie

Go on, get your Shine on!

PART 1: RIGHT HERE. RIGHT NOW.

I am writing this having had the news only a couple of hours ago that my dad has been diagnosed with prostate cancer. My initial reaction was shock so I felt numb because I literally didn't know what to think or feel. When I am lost for thought or feeling, the only thing I know how to do these days is to go within and ask my Spiritual Self, my Spiritual 'Team' and the Universe to guide me. I asked the Angels to be with Dad and give him all the loving, healing energy he needs. I asked the Universe to support him, to his highest will and good. The tears then came as my Spirit allowed me to connect with my feelings and I cried to the Spirit Realms to do everything possible to ensure Dad feels loved, safe and valued because ever since he was a child, he has never truly felt any of those things. My deepest wish is that Dad discovers he is loveable and valuable. To deeply feel it. To 'know' it. For me to feel deeply concerned for his emotional wellbeing and to physically feel the pain of his lack of belief in his own value is nothing short of miraculous. The anger, sadness, resentment and separateness I used to feel have been replaced with unconditional love, acceptance and understanding for him as a human being. Indeed, him as a Spirit. And I am grateful for the role he has played in my life because he has taught me so much.

I was reluctant to start writing as planned today, naturally. However, as I considered the topics I am about to cover, it hit me like a ton of bricks that my ability to feel such deep compassion and love for my dad is due to the miraculous work I am about to share with you. This work has been key to my new relationship with my father and this shift has been critical to truly setting myself free. Free to discover the truth of me and be a conscious, living expression of that.

Living Consciously

"If your mind carries a heavy burden of past, you will experience more of the same. The past perpetuates itself through lack of presence. The quality of your consciousness at this moment is what shapes the future." Eckharte Tolle

Consciousness as defined by my dictionary is:

> 1. the state of being <u>aware</u> of and <u>responsive</u> to one's surroundings
> 2. a person's awareness or perception of something
> * the fact of awareness by the mind of itself and the world.

The last exercise we did to witness your fear-based thoughts was a perfect example of what it means to live consciously. You were exercising your awareness muscle and that isn't a muscle many people use much. Daring & Mighty people use it a lot. We are ripped with awareness!

Noticing your thoughts, being honest about where you are at and how you truly feel is a conscious act. Most people find it very difficult to notice and then admit where they are emotionally unhappy in life. Being honest about your tough feelings can be scary. If you admit you are not happy in a particular area of your life, that could mean change and as we discovered earlier, change takes us out of our comfort zone, which can induce fear. Awareness could mean you discover that you are miserable at work. What do you do with that information?! Or awareness could mean you notice where your relationship isn't working. That knowledge could make you feel as if your world might crumble around you. Or it could mean you discover negative behavioural patterns you are running which are uncomfortable and embarrassing to admit to.

It takes the courage of a Super Hero to live in conscious awareness. It is not for the faint hearted. Developing this level of honesty with yourself takes bravery but once you master it, your life will become so wildly happy and fulfilled because you are living your truth. That gap between how you really feel and what you show to the world will become minuscule and it is so much easier to live like that. Keeping up appearances is exhausting! If what you show is what you are, the weight that is lifted off your shoulders will be life-changing. It just takes practice. All masters are obsessive about practice. Look at any sportsperson competing at an elite level – they practise all day every day. They are relentless. Their mind is on their end goal – to win. That is their motivation. Your motivation to change needs to outweigh your pain of staying the same and we will come to that very soon.

Living consciously is a choice. Up until now, you are likely to have been living predominantly unconsciously and yet you have survived. If you are surviving, you don't have to choose to alter things in your life. If you were threatened with death, you would do something about it. But you have been cruising along quite nicely in your comfort zone for some time, so why rock the boat?

Daring & Mighty people love to rock the boat because cruising is, quite frankly, boring. It's ok to slow down for a while here and there to re-group and nurture, but if you are cruising all day long, you would fall asleep! Conscious people are fully awake and present! In the words of the iconic British girl band, "SPICE up your life!" 'Slammin' to the left' and 'Shakin' to the right' is far from cruising! A bit of spice makes life worth living! If you have a gut feeling that things aren't quite as good as they could be, you have the choice to step up, take responsibility for your life (no one else is going to, nor should they) and decide what needs to change and how you are going to do that.

 *PUMP UP THE VOLUME!*

"Spice Up Your Life" - Spice Girls

Living consciously means you are not just surviving. Just surviving is dull. Anyone can just survive. Daring & Mighty people LIVE. We Dare to live our Mighty truth. Us humans are pure energy and energy is always changing. It's a fundamental universal law. We are changing every second. We can choose the direction of our change. We can choose to either expand or shrink. If you are living your truth then you are choosing to expand and grow. Growth feels great so we are motivated to keep doing it. The more we grow, the more we want to grow. The more we master living in awareness, the deeper our self-knowing becomes. Knowing yourself means greater clarity on what your special 'thing' is to contribute to the world. If you are not sharing your uniqueness with the world, it may as well not exist. What is the point of you if you are not sharing with the collective? Daring & Mighty people want to leave their mark on the world. The contribution of something unique and special is what they were put on this planet to do.

Living consciously is being aware of where you are now and where you want to be. The dictionary definition also states that consciousness is about being responsive to this awareness. So you need to DO something about it. Awareness is nothing without action and by the end of this book, you will have a lot of awareness and oodles of tools to help you put it into action. So stay tuned.

Staying on the Daring & Mighty path requires motivation, especially in the early days. You have already done some journalling on why you are reading this book and what it is in your life that simply has to change. And you made a promise to yourself to commit to a process that can assist you with this change. You have made a decision. Writing the story behind the decision is key to persisting with this work. Now I want you to take that a step further. Right here. Right now. I want you to acknowledge, with honesty and self-compassion, how you truly feel about your life. And we are going to do this by looking at the six human needs and how you rate for each one.

I was taught the six universal human needs by life coach and now friend,

Michelle Zelli. Michelle worked with Tony Robbins and learned these needs from him. I think the theory originated with the psychologist Abraham Maslow in 1943 and was adapted by Tony Robbins to become the human needs many coaches now refer to. Anyhow, these basic human needs are important to understand in terms of the ways in which we fulfill them (through both positive and negative behaviours) and how we rate their importance to us, as that very much defines who we are and how we behave. I will explain as simply as possible but if you want to hear one of Tony's many lectures on the topic, head on over to YouTube. His explanation of his updated model is powerful.

The first four fundamental human needs are requirements of our personality and they are needed for survival. The last two needs are requirements of our Spirit and they are needed for fulfillment. Daring & Mighty people aim to rate high with positive behaviours in all six areas. In a moment you will do an exercise to gauge how you are rating. If you rate high with negative behaviours or low or 'so so' generally, I will invite you to get real with where you are at and why. I will encourage you to get your rating off the Richter scale by choosing to do something about how you are fulfilling your basic needs. Why? Because I'm pretty sure that you desire to live an extraordinary life!

So let's have a look at the six needs. This is going to be a mixture of reading and exercises so get those pens and journals at the ready! The self-assessment work you are about to do can be profound. The more you put into this exercise the more you will get out and the better your foundation for the rest of our work together. So get pumped! While you are gathering your notepaper, listen to this tune because we are about to take a good look at where you are at, right here, right now.

PUMP UP THE VOLUME!

"Right Here. Right Now." - Fat Boy Slim

CERTAINTY

This is directly linked to our survival instinct and is the basis of our nervous system. We want to know that we are safe and secure, that our basic necessities of life are being met. So we need to have air, food, water, clothing and shelter. We need to ensure we are basically comfortable, avoiding pain and have a small amount of pleasure - preferably with some sex thrown in to propagate the species! In our western world, certainty means feeling SECURE because the meeting of our physiological needs are pretty much a given.

Positive behaviour that brings about certainty could be earning an income to ensure you are feeding, sheltering and clothing your family. Or perhaps a religious faith gives you certainty that you are fundamentally safe and held.

Negative behaviour that brings about certainty could be a tendency to control. 'Controlling' behaviour is a sure sign that certainty is of high importance to someone and usually means that another need rates correspondingly low. If attention was paid to the area that is likely to be sitting at 0 or 1, the control freak would probably chill out!

Where do you feel certain in your life? List everything that you are certain about. There could be some uncertain feelings alongside the certainty and that's ok - we will see why in a moment. You can still list certainty about something if at the same time you are experiencing uncertain feelings about the exact same thing.

On a scale of 1 - 10 (with 1 being very little certainty and 10 being absolute certainty), how do you rate the level of certainty in your life?

VARIETY

This keeps things interesting. If we knew all the answers and outcomes, we would be very bored! We need an element of mystery and surprise in our lives because that is what makes us grow. Variety fulfills us. We can get variety from the most simple things, such as learning something new, music, comedy or conversation. Tony Robbins says, *'The quality of your life is in direct proportion to the amount of uncertainty you can comfortably live with.'* If we can learn to get comfortable with uncertainty, then we are growing exponentially. We can't grow if we are not willing to take risks.

Positive behaviour that gives us uncertainty or variety could be starting a new business. You can discover your true passion by following your heart and taking a chance. By consciously deciding to take a leap of faith into the unknown, we discover an excitement for something new that encourages us to do it again. We develop certainty around creating uncertainty, which is the key to overcoming fear. We begin to witness that creating uncertainty can be the key to unlocking our true potential and we want to do more of it because it feels great!

Negative behaviour that creates uncertainty could be indulging in drugs and alcohol. We cannot guarantee our reactions and behaviours when under the influence of these and that gives us the uncertainty we need.

Where do you have uncertainty in your life? List everything you are uncertain about. As above, there could be some things that you are both uncertain and certain about. There is a power within those things.

On a scale of 1 - 10, how do you rate the level of variety (or uncertainty) in your life?

SIGNIFICANCE

We all need to feel special and that our life has meaning. We need to know that we are needed or important. Let's look at children for a moment. They need the certainty of a safe home and the uncertainty of adventurous storytelling or the excitement when unwrapping birthday presents. They equally need to know that they are unique and special. Children who are not told this suffer greatly as they grow into adulthood because they fundamentally do not feel significant. Feeling significant is required for survival so not telling a child that they are loved and important means they are in fear for their life. The younger the child, the more real their fear of not surviving is because they are literally dependent on their care-giver for survival. It really is as literal as that and as you will discover, this is a subject I am very passionate about!

Positive behaviour that gives us significance could be dressing well and receiving compliments, having a child and feeling important in their life, studying hard and being rewarded with a degree, being valued in your job, respected by your partner or giving to others, which makes you feel needed.

Negative behaviour that gives us significance might be playing the victim role - 'poor me' gets attention! Being the 'sick one' ensures attention too. The drama queen feels special because all focus is on her. In Australia we talk about the 'Tall Poppy Syndrome', which is a tendency to cut others down because their success makes us feel insignificant. We can make ourselves feel more significant by making the successful person appear less important.

Where do you feel significant in your life? List everything that makes you feel special and needed.

On a scale of 1 - 10, how do you rate the level of significance in your life?

LOVE / CONNECTION

We want to love and be loved. We want to feel a connectedness with others. Self-love is equally if not more critical. If you do not love yourself then you do not have the capacity or tools to love and connect with anyone else. Love and connection is the deepest need we have and possibly the toughest because it requires us to really open up and be vulnerable. The honesty, compassion and acceptance required to love ourselves is immense and that doesn't happen overnight. That is something to be practised and developed and there will be some exercises on this for you later in the book.

Positive behaviours that give us a feeling of love / connection might involve being moved by music and art. Daring to be vulnerable and committing to an honest and intimate relationship. Hugging your friends. Petting your cat! Bible study with fellow churchgoers. Connecting with nature - perhaps surfing is your thing, or walking in the woods.

Negative behaviours that give us a feeling of love / connection can be very similar to how we get significance. Being sick may ensure someone looks after you, making you feel loved. Being the victim with lots of issues to talk about ensures you are connecting with others. If they feel sorry for you, perhaps that makes you feel loved and cared for. Physical connection can be incredibly negative and violent. Think of the lyrics of 'Kiss with a Fist' by Florence & the Machine. "A kiss with a fist is better than none." Pretty stark, but sadly the negative attention gained from domestic violence does at least ensure attention, which can give the feeling of being loved. If you were taught at a young age that you were unloveable and the only way you got attention as that child was to be naughty and get a smack, it wouldn't be surprising to end up seeking love / connection in this way.

Where do you feel love / connection in your life? List everything that makes you feel loved and connected.

On a scale of 1 - 10, how do you rate the level of love / connection in your life?

Are you frightened of opening up to another person and showing your vulnerability? Is the idea of loving yourself totally foreign and weirding you out? Do you avoid joining social groups and clubs because you are not confident in making new friends? If you are rating quite low here, have a think about where you could be compensating. Are you focusing your energy on having certainty? Variety? Significance? All three? Remember, awareness is the first step towards change. This exercise wasn't designed to give you permission to beat yourself up but I do want you to get in touch with the truth of where you are at and feel it. If it is painful, allow yourself to feel it with compassion and understanding. Soon we will look at why you have set up your life the way you have – there will be good reason. For now, please just witness it with love.

At this point it is also worth considering who your peer group is because the people we seek love / connection from can greatly influence the decisions we make and the lives we lead. Remember, you have a choice in everything. You can choose who you want to connect with. This means you can choose people on the same wave-length as you, with the same standards, moral and ethical codes. You can even choose to connect with people who inspire you to be better. Why spend time with people who influence you to be a lesser version of yourself? They can't make you 'be' or 'do' anything but if you crave connection with someone, the quickest way to getting it is by being like them.

You make that choice, largely subconsciously, because this is what you learned as a child. The survival instinct of a very young child says, "If I behave like them, they will love me." A toddler believes she will secure her parents' love by being like them. She needs to be loved by them to ensure her survival. We will learn much more about this soon. For now, have a think about who you are spending time with. Are there people in your life that you seek connection from and who are influencing you to be a smaller version of yourself? You give power to your peers. If you are happy to be influenced by them, give them that power.

Remember, this is in your control. As you gain confidence in your Daring & Mighty self, do not be surprised if your peer group alters somewhat.

Ok, so that is a basic explanation of the first four needs and these are the ones we must have to survive. As you saw, there can be both positive and negative ways to meet those needs. Now we will move away from survival to fulfillment. These are the needs of our Spirit and this is where us Daring & Mighty peeps get really excited. This is where the fun happens!

GROWTH

You are a Spirit in a Body. You are a Soul having a human experience. Your Spirit by its very nature is a creative being. All it knows is to evolve and grow. That is your purpose for having this human experience - to remember the truth of your Soul and have a unique experience in this lifetime. The goal of your Spirit is for you to live a life that is a full expression of the truth of you. Some say you will keep coming back and having multiple human experiences until you finally experience and express the full truth of who you are. It has been said that to not grow equates death. Well, certainly it is the death of your Spirit if you deny it the purpose of its existence!

When we speak of growth we mean in the areas of self-development and self-fulfillment. You are learning about who you really are and what makes you tick. You are discovering your values and what you like to do to feel that you are truly expressing who you are. If you are fundamentally a creative, are you expressing that? If you are an adventurous spirit, are you expressing that? If you are deeply motivated by fitness, how is that being reflected in your life? Does your Spirit crave to learn and are you nourishing your soul by reading, attending courses and workshops? If you know in your gut you were put on this earth to learn about love, what are you doing to connect with and express that truth? Does the work you do offer you challenge and growth? How about your relationships? Do you feel as if your life is evolving?

Where are you experiencing growth in your life?

On a scale of 1 - 10, how do you rate the level of growth in your life?

CONTRIBUTION

When we develop the ability to properly fulfill all our basic human needs and know that our Spirit is growing and evolving, there is a very natural desire and perhaps even compulsion to contribute to the lives of others. If our cup is full, indeed if our cup runneth over, we do not want to waste anything. Rather, we want to share that juicy goodness with others and that feels great. It is essentially what being human is all about. We are no good to others though unless we are helping ourselves first. That is the point of getting the first five needs sorted – then we are able to be of service to others. When I was stuck in a victim head-space and suffering anxiety, I was far from able to help anyone else! When I woke up, did the work and started to fill my human needs cups healthily, I was compelled to help others.

I know I say we have a choice in everything but in this area, I feel the choice is taken away. It's like we have no choice but to serve because it becomes the most natural thing to do. It's automatic. It's almost as if we have come full circle and are back to basic survival mode. At this point, if I am not serving, I am dying. And interestingly, Tony Robbins says, *'Anything that doesn't contribute gets eliminated – whether it's an appendage or a species,'* and I totally get that. If we are not contributing, we may as well be eliminated.

When our five cups are full, the spillover goes to others because we suddenly become aware that it's not all about me! It's about us. The penny drops and suddenly we really 'get it'! Energetically we are all one and this is the meaning of life. To serve. Right....there you have it. You heard it here first! The meaning of life. Tick. You can go home now! LOL.

Where are you experiencing contribution in your life?

On a scale of 1 - 10, how do you rate the level of contribution in your life?

Having completed the exercises around the six human needs, how are you feeling? May I challenge you a step further? If you rated yourself a 5 in any area and feel *comfortable* but know in your gut that you could be happier, please think harder about this one. I want you to push those brain muscles and get in touch with what you are not happy about and bring that number down. Yes, DOWN. Don't sit in the no man's land of a 5. The more you can access your unhappiness in this area, the more honest you are being – which will drive you to want to do something about it. Feeling 'fine' is NOT Daring & Mighty. If you don't feel fabulous, then figure out why. Feel why. Motivate yourself to change!

I hope you have found these exercises interesting and I hope you have discovered something new about yourself. I find that learning about these human needs not only helps me to align my own life and make changes to ensure optimum fulfillment but also to notice what might be going on for someone else and having compassion and understanding for why they might behave the way they do. Rather than labelling someone a control freak or an egomaniac, I am able to consider what could really be going on for them and think of them with compassion rather than judgement. Getting in touch with my own 'stuff' certainly takes the focus off others and theirs! Giving myself compassion and understanding equally helps me to give that to others. And this is an ongoing learning process.

You have just done a lot of work and I hope you feel you have given it your 100%. Really getting in touch with where you are at - Right Here. Right Now. - that is what will motivate you to change. This is a task that no one but you can do and that takes courage and persistence. So I want to congratulate you! And I want you to give yourself a big pat on the back. Go on!!

And now it's time for a big HUG!! And a song! And an affirmation! Woohoo!

PUMP UP THE VOLUME!

"Don't Worry. Be Happy" - Juice Music, Scott Aplin, Phil Bart

This song is so lovely and lighthearted and I figure you need a bit of that right now.

While you are listening to this, give yourself a big hug. Remember I said that hugging yourself was going to become normal? Well, it's time to start! You can sit and close your eyes and listen to the song with your arms wrapped around yourself. Close yourself into a ball with your arms if you really want to feel safe. Or, if you are feeling lifted and lighthearted, dance about the room but make sure those arms are wrapped about you. It may feel odd to start with but please give it a go. It really does feel good to acknowledge yourself and show love, support and safety to yourself. Don't worry! Be Happy! Hug yourself!

I am... YOUR AFFIRMATION

I notice where I am at, right here, right now, with compassion and love.

Your Conscious Dream

"All our dreams come true if we have the courage to pursue them."
Walt Disney

What is it that your heart desires? I don't mean material things at this point. I mean what does your heart and soul yearn for? If you could be, do or feel anything of your choosing, what would it look like? What work would you do? What kind of relationships would you have? Where would you live? Who would you spend time with? How would you feel about yourself? How would you spend your free time? How much free time do you have?! How are you expressing your soul?

I bet you have to stop and think carefully about these questions. Do the answers come to you rapidly, with crystal clear clarity?! I am going to take a punt and suggest that you are having to really stop and think about these answers. That perhaps you don't even really know what your answers might be? Do you know why? It's because most of us focus far too much on what we don't have! We seem to be able to see very clearly what is not in front of us! Surely that is a Super Power and a good thing?! Well, no. But it does demonstrate that we have the Super Human ability to vision something that isn't there. It is our choice (woah, there's that word again!!) whether we vision what we don't have or what we *expect* to have. Expect is a great word here (she says, patting herself on the back...and enjoying the feeling of significance!) – there is immense power in that word because with expectation comes a deep belief in the power within and around you that WILL support and co-create your vision. You command it. You expect it. In Part 3 – My Vision. My Future. – we are going to be doing a lot of work on visioning and manifesting. You will learn to harness Universal Laws and your own power to bring into reality your deepest desires. For now, I would like you to be open to the idea that you can have anything you want. And you can feel any way you want. Visioning is a tool for getting you there.

I love the work by Dr. Joe Dispenza on this topic. He is a biochemist, neuroscientist and chiropractor with postgraduate training in neurology, neuroscience, brain function and chemistry, cellular biology, memory formations, aging and longevity. The man is a scientist! And he knows his stuff.

Dr. Joe explains and shows how the brain can literally re-wire itself. We can choose what we want to think, what we want to feel, the life that we want to create, and the brain will re-wire accordingly. Our brain doesn't know the difference between what we see in front of us and what we imagine. What we imagine, the brain interprets as the truth. So when we focus on what we don't have, our brain believes that we do not have these things and that affects our thoughts and behaviours, which bring about this truth in our lives. Equally, when we focus on what we want or expect to have, again our brain interprets this as the truth and rewires to affect our thoughts and behaviours, which co-creates this truth.

I think Dr Joe is the best and most qualified to explain how thinking in new ways, as well as changing beliefs, can literally rewire one's brain. The following is detailed on his website:

The premise of his work is founded in his total conviction that every person on this planet has within them the latent potential of greatness and true unlimited abilities.

Dr Dispenza explains that you are not doomed by your genes and hardwired to be a certain way for the rest of your life. A new science is emerging that empowers all human beings to create the reality they choose.

Hear, hear!

So far we have done a lot of work to connect with and gain awareness of where we are right now. Now I want you to do a short exercise to begin building an awareness of where you want to be. I want you to start to build a vision to work towards. This is a beautiful exercise. Let your imagination run wild! Be brave and admit to yourself what you really want. Enjoy!!

 *AN EXERCISE*

This is a free flowing writing exercise. Write anything and everything that comes into your head. Most importantly, write what you want as if you already have it. So your sentences start with *I have* and *I am* and *I enjoy* and *I love* etc. Don't censor this. What inner nudges have you been refusing to acknowledge? Pay them attention now and write them down. If money, people's opinions, judgements and fear were not factors, what would you want to be, do or have? Consider these areas of your life as thought starters:

> physical health / fitness
>
> money / finance
>
> relationships with family / friends / colleagues
>
> relationship with partner
>
> career / work
>
> spirituality / religion
>
> adventure
>
> learning
>
> contribution
>
> feelings / emotions

Connect with how you will FEEL when you have what you want. For example,

> "I feel so excited to have work that allows me to express my creativity and I love that my work makes other people happy!"
>
> "I love my husband deeply. Our relationship is intimate,

respectful and easy. I feel so loved and blessed!"

"I feel light and free. I love myself. Life no longer feels so hard and I bloody love being comfortable in my own skin!"

"I have a stable bank balance and total financial security. I know that all my regular expenses are covered and it feels so good to enjoy the freedom I have to spend money whenever and however I like. I love feeling wealthy!"

"I love running 5 miles 3 times a week. I feel invigorated and alive. I am at the perfect weight and I am so proud of myself. I always knew I could do it!"

"I have one day every week completely to myself and I love that I get to choose whatever I want to do with it. I enjoy volunteering at the local hospice, horse-riding, painting, meditating and going to the spa!"

Don't forget to describe your vision using all of your senses. I really want you to experience it as if you are there, amongst it. So if you are talking about your home, detail it. Describe the light and the location. Who are your neighbours? What is inside your house? Is it filled with pets and plants and muddy football boots? Are there touchy feely rugs, cushions and blankets? How have you decorated? What colours do you see? What sounds do you hear? Is your dog barking in the garden and has your daughter got her stereo blaring in her dream loft bedroom?

Do you have something that you have always wanted to achieve in your life? Do you watch documentaries of people exploring untouched parts of the planet and wish you could do that too? Perhaps you want to write a play? Or bake that gateau! Remember all your dreams? Write them here!

Get as detailed as you can. The bigger you make your dream now, the bigger the goal you have to work towards. Get emotionally attached to your vision. Get excited and enjoy the process. How often, as adults, do we get to dream?

 *PUMP UP THE VOLUME!*

"Don't Stop Me Now!" - Queen

This is a GREAT song for visioning!! Don't stop!

I am... *YOUR AFFIRMATION*

I expect my dreams to come true!

Your Conscious Nightmare

How do you feel having got conscious about your dreams? Did you build a big vision? I trust it was sufficiently Daring & Mighty!? Remember, we want that dream to sustain you through some of the learning we are about to embark on, which is going to really challenge you and stretch those brain muscles! Not to mention your awareness muscles! When you feel like giving up, remember your vision. Surely your dreams are worth fighting for?!

Now we are going to get conscious about what isn't working for you right now. This is essentially an extension of the six human needs exercise. We are going to build awareness around where you are dissatisfied in your life. How far is your world right now from the vision you just wrote? Again, this is not an opportunity to give yourself a hard time. Hopefully you are starting to see that we are building a true picture of where you are at, with compassion and love. This is another exercise in awareness.

But first, let's take a look at what dissatisfaction actually is. I bet you have always thought that dissatisfaction was a negative thing. Perhaps it is for the majority. For the elite few people on the Daring & Mighty path, it is quite the opposite. For us, it's a signpost to growth. You know how you always wanted someone to just tell you what to do next? Someone to show you your purpose? To lay it out for you and tell you when to take action and how? Well, that miraculous person has just turned up! Yippee! Remember when we looked at the human need of growth and we discovered that you are a Spirit in a Body? That you are a Soul having a human experience? Well, it is that Spirit within you that can give you all your answers.

Aw, I know you were hoping that a wise magical fairy was going to burst through your door, parchment roll in hand, and declare proudly the purpose of your life with step-by-step instructions! Hmmm, not quite.

But it's something similar! Believe me when I tell you that when you choose to meet your Spirit self and allow your life to be guided by that voice, it's just as if you do have your own inner guidance system showing you the way. It's not as easy as step-by-step instructions but that would mean too much certainty! Remember, to survive we need a nice healthy balance of certainty and uncertainty. We would be so bored if we were given instructions. The key to loving your life is embracing the adventure, the unknown, the wonderment. Gosh, if we did have a fairy with our own personal instruction manual, I wouldn't be writing this book and life would be robotic. We would have nothing to dream about! Booooring!

Our Spirit breathes life into us and navigates us gently and lovingly through our human experience. You can choose to have a human experience that feels hard, out of control and off radar. Or you can choose to tune into your creative being, whose purpose is to remind you of your truth and show you how to express that. Your Spirit can show you the way, if you choose to listen.

Dissatisfaction is a gift because it is a message from your Spirit, telling you it's time to grow! If the dissatisfaction in a particular area of your life is really uncomfortable, then that's a great big signpost telling you something isn't working and it's time to try something else. It's time to take a leap of faith, spread those gorgeous wings of yours and fly! And remember, taking flight will get easier and easier as you build more and more evidence in the existence of your Spirit and your own marvellous capabilities. As we have already learned, you will become certain in your uncertainty!

To be clear, you could be feeling rather happy with your life but that doesn't mean you will not still experience dissatisfaction. Dissatisfaction's job is to push you to grow. It's a powerful motivator, forcing you to create goals and achieve them - which means you are moving forward.

Even the most seemingly successful, happy people feel dissatisfaction.

We are all looking for fulfillment in all areas of life. You could have oodles of cash, international fame, a ridiculously happy family and adventurous holidays yet feel dissatisfied with your lot because you are lacking a sense of spirituality and contribution. Perhaps you are craving to learn something new or you really could do with losing a few kilos! There is always some aspect of your Spirit that needs expression. We are never completely cooked. Even the most enlightened among us are still growing. We never stop.

So what feels like a nightmare for you? Where are you stuck? Where do you feel annoyed, angry, disappointed, irritated, resentful, frustrated, restless, disapproving, disgusted, regretful or dismayed? Those are all words from the dictionary to describe dissatisfaction, by the way. And trust me, as you tune into your Spirit and live committedly on the Daring & Mighty path, the way you experience dissatisfaction will alter and become more gentle. Mostly because you are not ignoring it, letting it fester and get nasty. You are paying it attention!

 *AN EXERCISE*

Let's identify where you are feeling dissatisfied.

If we go back to the same areas of your life around which you wrote your vision, we will start to witness the distance between where you are now and where you want to be. When you look at each area of your life, do the following:

Rate your dissatisfaction out of 10 (1 being very little, 10 being highly dissatisfied).

Consider the impact any dissatisfaction is having on your life. How is the dissatisfaction in one area of your life affecting the other areas?

What will your life look like if you do nothing about the dissatisfaction?

Get emotionally involved with how your dissatisfaction really feels. It's important to have an emotional experience of this new awareness.

With regard to your feelings / emotions, consider here the feelings or behaviours that you don't feel you have control over / how you deal with pain in your life / how you behave when you are angry / how you behave when you are feeling flat or depressed / how you react or respond to situations.

Give yourself at least an hour to look at all of the following areas. Remember, the more you put into this work, the more you will get out and it is SO worth it!

physical health / fitness

money / finance

relationships with family / friends / colleagues

relationship with partner

career / work

spirituality / religion

adventure

learning

contribution

feelings / emotions

Well done for completing that task. It's a big one!

Now answer the following questions:

1. Which area(s) of your life rated the highest?

2. Where are you feeling the *impact* the most?

3. Was the area that rated highest expected? Or was it a surprise?

4. If you think about what friends, family, colleagues mostly criticise you for, can you see any links to where you are experiencing dissatisfaction?

5. Did you have any physical reactions while doing this exercise?

6. What do you think are your biggest challenges - the things you would most like to change in your life?

7. How far are you from your conscious dream that you wrote about earlier? How does this make you feel?

Take a moment to absorb how you are feeling having answered all those questions. Let it all sink in for a while.

Are you feeling more determined than ever to understand your dissatisfactions and why you are where you are? Or are you feeling defeated? Whatever you feel is ok. Just don't give up! Keep going. Chaos comes before change and in my experience, feeling really rubbish means that very soon, just around the corner, there will be a breakthrough!

Let's shelve all your answers for now. Let it be and let this all sink in. We will come back to this and the answers you need will slowly come to you. For now, it's really important to connect to the emotions you experienced while doing this exercise. May I suggest you sit quietly with your eyes closed and listen to the wise words of the Beatles. Please do yourself a favour and absorb all you have just uncovered. Music can very kindly and gently help you to do this.

 *PUMP UP THE VOLUME!*

"Let It Be" - The Beatles

I am... YOUR AFFIRMATION

I welcome the voice of my Spirit and allow it to guide and support me. I spread my beautiful wings of growth!

Who is the Captain of Your Life?

The other day my six-year-old son asked me, "Mummy, are you the captain of your work?" He perceives a captain to be like the captain of a fire station or the captain of a pirate ship. The commander, leader or master. I said I was and that felt good to say because not only am I my own boss, more importantly my work allows me to express my truth. To be the captain of my truth - to have mastered myself in order to feel the way I do now is what I wish for everyone. To be the captain of your life means becoming conscious of what does not serve you and letting that stuff go. It means you are living in a vibration of love and abundance. You feel completely on purpose. You love yourself and you love your life.

"To be nobody but yourself in a world that's doing its best to make you somebody else, is to fight the hardest battle you are ever going to fight. Never stop fighting." E.E. Cummings

The E.E. Cummings quote above is brilliant. Read it again and absorb those wonderful words. This is what being Daring & Mighty is all about. Daring & Mighty people never stop fighting to be themselves because in their gut they know the truth of them is worth fighting for. As Spirits having a human experience, they know they have chosen this human existence for a reason - to remember who they are, unveil their truth and grow as a result. Overcoming 'being human' allows the evolution of their Soul. The paradox is that while remembering our truth we must still 'be human' because that is what we are and for particularly evolved souls, this can be a tough lesson in itself. Overcoming 'being human' is to recognise that life experiences, the family, religion and culture we are born into, the teachers we have, the body we have been given and so forth all challenge the true expression of our Spirit.

When we are very young, we are not aware that our Spirit is being challenged. In fact, all we are aware of is that we are very basically dependent on others for survival. We need to be loved and in its most simple terms that means being protected, clothed, sheltered and fed. Our only perceived challenge is survival. It is at this stage of life (psychologists tend to agree it is between the ages of 0 - 7) that we are most *susceptible* to the challenge of being human and it is at this time that the shrouding of our Spirit begins. Our truth is cloaked in a rich tapestry of lessons we need to learn. We unwittingly learn to be like our carers – after all, if we are like them, surely that will secure their attention and perhaps they will even love us. The mind of a child innocently believes that to copy its carers (usually parents) assures its survival. And so we take on beliefs and behaviours that are not inherently ours - except they were 'destined' to become ours, because at a Soul level, we chose the family we were born into, assuring us of the perfect 'shroud'. A bespoke shroud that would ensure we were challenged magnificently. A shroud that had the potential, if we would only see it, to be a gift of growth. If we can see the challenges and choose to learn from them, we are gifted with the evolution of our Soul.

So imagine yourself wearing a coat of the most intricate, delicate, complex design, woven in a myriad of colours, multiple layers and textures. Every tangled thread, every serpentine knit, every twist and fold of fabric represents a behaviour or belief or emotional state that has weighed you down and challenged you throughout your life. You have worn this coat since you were very young and it has become more elaborate, torturous and heavy as you have grown. Even the most enlightened, conscious, loving parents will mould a child in a particular way. No one but you knows your Spirit and knows its true expression. No one but you can make the decision to take the reins, lighten your load and be YOU.

You have the choice to grow out of this coat or to be swamped by it. You have the choice to evolve from an uncomfortable state of survival or remain burdened, allowing layer upon layer of challenging behaviours and beliefs to continue to enshroud you.

You can choose to re-create your life. One thread at a time, you can unravel and understand the lessons you were sent here to learn. The goal is to release the burdening weight of that coat and to feel light and free and truly yourself. To stand strong and lovingly empowered. Because you are unique and just perfect.

To be clear, some of the beliefs and behaviours of others may now be quirks that you rather like about yourself. Here we are looking at those qualities that are not serving you. And we are looking without judgement because this is nobody's fault. It is likely that negative qualities we have taken on from others - largely our parents - were adopted from their parents and theirs from their parents and so on. It's a generational cycle. It is what it is. This happens. To everyone.

A Daring & Mighty person decides to journey to their centre, to discover who they really are. They are brave because they must dig through so many layers to get to that truth and uncovering each layer can be incredibly painful, depending on your story. They battle on. They never stop the fight to discover who they are. They break the mould!

So far you have done a lot of work to uncover your fears and negative internal chatter. You know how fulfilled you feel in life by looking at your six basic human needs and where you are feeling deeply dissatisfied. We have compared these inner truths and the reality of your life now with the life you deeply want to live and the way you really want to feel. We have already gained immense awareness around negative behavioural patterns and belief systems you have and how these are being reflected in your day to day life. Now it's time to begin to understand, without blame, how we have adopted these behaviours largely from our parents. Up until now, you may have thought that you have no control over what triggers you. That you have no control over the type of life you are experiencing. Well, you do. You have a CHOICE. You can be and feel anything you choose. You can choose behaviour that feels true to you. You can love yourself completely. You can feel a sense of inner peace and quiet.

The key to unlocking the truth of you is finding compassion, forgiveness and acceptance for yourself as you are, right now. It is also about forgiveness for those from whom you have inherited the beliefs and behaviours that are not serving you. That forgiveness allows you to live in a much more forgiving, compassionate, easy way. Discovering your Spirit and learning to be guided by that voice is your ticket to forgiveness and living a deeply fulfilled life. When we develop a relationship with our Spirit, we can hand over control to its awesome and loving energy - an energy that can heal any wound and forgive anyone. An energy that can transform your life and co-create any dream.

In your gut, I bet you just know that the key to a complete life, inside and out, is love. Am I right? Even if the idea of loving yourself seems foreign to you, it was a sense of love for yourself that guided you to pick up this book because you want something better for yourself. Perhaps something is telling you that the way you relate to and treat others may not be 100% loving? That if you were motivated by love, your relationships would be better? You are right. Love is our essence. It is what connects us, internally and externally. And we all know it at some deep level.

You have been motivated by love since the day you were born. As we have just discovered, you sought the love of your parents because that secured your basic survival requirements. However, as I am sure you know, the healthiest, happiest babies are those who are shown affection and love. Although a baby can probably survive without love, it certainly will not thrive. A bit like us as adults - we can survive alone and without connection, but we will not flourish. We are hardwired to connect with other human beings. At the very least, connection ensures procreation. But it is so much more than that. We are all one. To cut off from others is like cutting off a limb. A part of us dies. A child that does not receive unconditional love must surely feel as if something inside has died and that feeling remains inside them for the rest of their life. Can you relate to that feeling? Certainly that feeling of something missing or cut off inside me is what led me on a self-development journey and ironically, I was a very loved child!

It was the negative behavioural patterns that I witnessed in my parents that caused me to feel cut off from them at some level. Their depression, anxiety and addictive behaviours - although very well covered up - reached me at an unconscious, intuitive level. Babies are still pure Spirit so their intuitive radar is on full beam. At some level, I felt the love from my parents as conditional. That wasn't their fault. They would be horrified at the suggestion that this was true. They simply loved me the best they could but my intuition told me that something wasn't quite right - that they weren't really 'happy' and perhaps that was my fault in some way. If I behaved a different way then perhaps everything would be ok. And bam! There was a perceived condition placed on their love. That condition caused me to feel cut off, hence that little black hole inside me which I always sensed but didn't understand.

If you were not getting your parents' attention - perhaps they were busy with their work, or perhaps they were 'there but not there' due to depression or other mental illness - you likely grew up believing you must be worthless. "You are always working so I must not be worth your time. I am worthless." As an adult, the belief 'I am worthless' will subconsciously guide every thought, feeling and behaviour.

If you were not feeling your parents' love - perhaps they had died, abandoned you or they displayed a lot of anger towards you - you probably grew up believing you were not loveable.

At some level, a belief that love is conditional means you grow up incapable of having a healthy flow of love in your life - for yourself, for others and from others.

Being cut off at this level from your parents means you will carry that void forever, unless it is recognised and understood. Those feelings of not being good enough, of being worthless, unloveable, self-conscious, fearful - or whatever your story - will stick with you throughout your life, making you feel incredibly uncomfortable because more often than not they will cause you to behave in ways that are simply not true to you. Your behaviour feels inappropriate in some way and not understanding why, feeling out of control and not knowing how to change it can be so frustrating.

When you are your most uncomfortable, you are probably either expressing the most negative of your parents' behaviours or rebelling against them. How often do we say, "OMG, I sound just like my mother!" Or "I will never treat my kids the way my dad treated me."

The anger around such discomfort was the push I needed to do something about it. I had to escape the cycle and address the root of all that triggered me. I had to become the captain of my life because quite frankly, although I was a grown woman who had not lived at home since the age of 17, my feelings and behaviours demonstrated that my parents were unwittingly running the show.

If our parents knew how to love themselves unconditionally with complete understanding, forgiveness and compassion then that is what we would have learned. If they were able to love others and be loved healthily, we would have learned that. If they had healthy boundaries, so would we. If they knew their job as parents was to nurture and encourage the expression of our soul, then we would be living our loving truth.

 *PUMP UP THE VOLUME!*

"Children" - Sarah Warwick with Peter Coyte & Malcolm Stern - Songs from Kahlil Gibran's 'The Prophet' Vol. 1

Close your eyes and listen to this beautiful song. Focus on yourself as a small child - a pure Spirit.

I am... YOUR AFFIRMATION

I am worthy and loveable. My soul is pure.

AN EXERCISE - Part 1

Let's take a look at the beliefs and attitudes that shape you. This is a big exercise and again, the more time you put into this, the more awareness you will gain. I would suggest this exercise will take at *least* a couple of hours. Perhaps chunk it down into manageable portions. In fact, not rushing and allowing some time to digest this exercise will give you far greater insights and understandings.

We are going to go back to the 10 areas of your life we examined in the 'Your Vision' and 'Dissatisfaction' exercises.

When we talk in this exercise about parents, please consider any carers - people who played a parental role in your life.

We will start by looking at your parents' beliefs, attitudes and behaviours - both positive and negative. When you answer the questions below, not only list their beliefs, but list how they would verbalise or demonstrate them. What messages do they give, both spoken and unspoken? For example, around the area of money, perhaps a parent repeated phrases such as "Do you think I'm made of money?" or "We can't afford it." Perhaps actions spoke louder than words and a parent was particularly generous and comfortable with spending money - there was an unspoken certainty that there was always more than enough money in your household.

To be clear, you may have an excellent relationship with your parents. Anything holding you back in life, however, will link to beliefs and behaviours you have inherited that are not authentically yours. If you are being held back, you likely have a tie to your parents or carers in some way. This process is all about standing separate from your parents and healthily claiming your life as your own. It's part of growing up. We all have to do it some day!

Please answer each of the following for Mum, Dad (and carers if relevant to you). Consider them individually rather than grouping them together.

Physical Health / Fitness:

What relationship did your parents have towards their body, health, fitness and food?

Money / Finance:

What relationship did your parents have towards money / finance?

Relationships with Family / Friends / Colleagues:

How did your parents interact with other people?

Relationship with Partner:

How did your parents interact with each other? (How would you describe their friendship, sexuality, partnership, romance?)

Career / Work:

What were your parents' attitudes toward career and work?

Spirituality / Religion:

What were your parents' opinions around religion and spirituality?

Adventure:

Was adventure a part of your parents' lives?

Learning:

Did your parents have opinions around learning and education? What kind of learning did they undertake?

Contribution:

Did your parents contribute to society in any particular way?

Feelings / Emotions:

Can you give a general description of your parents' emotional normality? How do you think they mostly felt? Were they mostly happy and joyful? Adventurous? Playful? Rebellious? Anxious? Fearful? Ashamed?

How did they behave when they were angry?

How about when they were down or depressed? Or in pain?

Do you know how they dealt with their emotions?

Do you think they were in control of them? If not, what emotions were they not in control of?

 *AN EXERCISE - Part 2*

Now let's have a look at what you have taken on as your own - there will be good stuff and stuff that isn't serving you. Carefully go through the beliefs and attitudes you have listed of your parents and highlight the ones you know you also have to some extent which are NOT serving you. Whether you wholeheartedly agree with a belief or only a tiny amount, highlight it.

While going through this exercise you will be digging deeper into your subconscious and you may discover more beliefs that you share with one or both parents that you hadn't previously listed. Write that under the appropriate heading and highlight it. Don't forget to highlight things that you know you rebel against too! If you find yourself flatly denying that you share a behaviour, look again! Perhaps a behavioural habit of denial is covering over the actual existence of a behaviour you are really uncomfortable about admitting to yourself.

This is a really tough exercise. There is no getting away from that. It takes such courage and persistence to get the most out of this. Remember, you are now Daring & Mighty! That means the truth is your goal. You WILL get to the other side. You will feel free. Stay with it! Choose to be the captain of your life.

 *AN EXERCISE - Part 3*

Now consider what the people in your life might criticise you for. What does your partner, family, friends, colleagues say about you? Do any of these match any of your parents' behaviours or beliefs? If so, highlight them. You may not like to believe that you carry these traits, but if others are noticing them, they are probably with you to some extent. If you don't know what others really think of you, perhaps be really brave and ask them? Ask people you deeply trust to give you loving and honest feedback. Try not to be defensive. Just listen. You never know, you could deepen some friendships as a result of such vulnerability. And don't be discouraged if someone doesn't want to highlight your 'stuff'. It's a challenging request for them, just as much as it can be challenging to receive the feedback.

Once you have done this, go through all the highlighted words and list them out separately. You will end up with a long list of behaviours and beliefs that can now sit consciously within your awareness. Some may be a surprise. Many will not. Sit with this awareness. Consider how this has all been playing out in your life. Know that with this awareness, you will start to see these traits as clear as day as you go about your daily routine. You will likely feel even more uncomfortable now that you are able to consciously witness them in action. That's ok. Remember that you are so much more than the stuff you have inherited from your parents! You are a beautiful Spirit and she will be shining so much more brightly once you clear away these layers.

As with all our exercises, please keep exercising those self-love muscles with compassion and understanding. Remember, awareness is our goal here and as a Daring & Mighty person you are a silent observer. Keep up that honesty - you will be rewarded.

You have done SO much work and I want to honour you and your commitment to this process. It is bloody hard and bloody exhausting and you are doing SO well to get this far. Believe me, the rest of the book is NOT going to be nearly as much work nor as tough as this first part. You know, as I write this I am remembering my process of discovery around what I had adopted from my parents. It was a mammoth undertaking but I was being driven by the most powerful force - the desire to change. I was so effing fed up with not feeling authentically 'me' that I was literally willing to do anything to do something about it! I put hours and hours of work into these exercises and was so well rewarded for my efforts. When I finished my rather confronting list I felt as if I had been dragged through a hedge backwards. I was totally overwhelmed, numb, embarrassed, annoyed that I had 'allowed' my parents' 'stuff' to control my life, angry, resentful and ripped off that I had spent so much of my precious life living and behaving in a way that was not serving me and I was left wondering, who am I? Seriously, if I am NOT all of this 'stuff', then who the hell am I?

"Nature abhors a vacuum." Aristotle

Aristotle observed that nature requires space to be filled with something, even if it is unseen, colourless, odourless air. I am telling you this because that is what you are doing right now. As I said, when I finished the same exercises as you are doing now, I wondered who I was without the 'stuff' that had defined me for so many years. And this is something to consider right now. But first, let me point out that you are not your 'stuff'. Your 'stuff' is what you do. Not fundamentally who you are. That said, I know from experience that it can feel like you don't know who you are or how to behave if you let go of what isn't serving you. As you become aware of some traits, just that awareness will disappear them away. Truly! The bigger, more stubborn ones needs some work, and we will get to that. When our 'stuff' starts to disappear, we create a void or a vacuum. This WILL be filled with something. It is a Universal Law. The crucial thing now is that you choose what to replace it with. Say you stop smoking. A lot of people complain that they put on weight after quitting that habit. That's because they chose to eat instead of smoke. This decision may have been unconscious but they did make a choice.

Now, as a Daring & Mighty, consciously aware adult, you can consciously choose what you fill your void with. As we progress into the next section of the book, you will start to connect to your true Spiritual Self. You will start to see that you are not your behavioural patterns, that you are your Spirit Self.

For now, consciously choose to replace any feelings of emptiness or loss with love. When in doubt, choose love! Daring & Mighty love!

If at any point you are on your knees and don't know what to do, send a prayer out to the Universe and ask that love guide you. If you fear being lost and unknown without your parents' negative beliefs and behaviours, just ask that love replace them. If you feel like you can't continue to dig any deeper into discovering your 'stuff', ask love to help you. Know in your heart that love is the answer. Love will guide you to your truth and ensure you fill the void with something that will serve you, to your highest will and good.

I want to reward you now with a fab song and affirmation. I want you to congratulate yourself on the work you have done so far. Meditate on these words. Dance around the room! Express the energy that is inside you. 'Dog Days Are Over' by Florence & The Machine is such a powerful song and I am sure it has many interpretations. When I first heard it, I had just completed these exercises so all of that information was bubbling about in my head. When it came on the radio, I just knew it was a message to me that my 'dog days' were over. I interpreted the words to mean that if I was brave enough to leave my mother and father's traits behind, happiness would hit me 'like a train on a track'. That once I had freed myself, there would be 'no turning back'. That I no longer needed to cover up my uncomfortable feelings with 'drink' and 'kisses'. I no longer needed to hide 'around corners' and 'under beds'. The guiding and reassuring voice of the Universe never ceases to amaze me – and I just love that it can choose funky music to speak to us when we need to hear it most!

 *PUMP UP THE VOLUME!*

"Dog Days Are Over" - Florence & The Machine

I am...
YOUR AFFIRMATION

I am not my parents' 'stuff'. I am unique and special. Step by step, day by day, I am creating my True Self.

I want to encourage you to do a little more work on discovering all that is not serving you. If you need to do a little bit every day, do that. There is no rush. There is no right or wrong. The key is putting in your best effort. It isn't about getting it perfect. It's about having an emotional experience that is true to you. You know what is right for you. You will know when you feel you have done the work you need to do. Trust that.

AN EXERCISE - Part 5

This is a free writing exercise. I would like you to journal how you feel having created your list. Make this writing really emotional. Really connect to how you feel. Again, there is no right or wrong. What you feel is right for you. Write about what is getting in the way of who you really are.

Take a look again at the 10 areas of your life and write about how taking on your parents' 'stuff' has negatively affected each area. Notice if the areas of your life that you earlier identified as your greatest dissatisfaction are linked to beliefs you have adopted from your parents.

Finish up this writing task with writing how badly you want to be the captain of your own life. If you could free yourself of your parents' behaviours, who would you be? Work those visioning muscles hard - what is the best version of yourself that you want to experience every day?

Get excited to be that person because she is waking up right NOW!

 *PUMP UP THE VOLUME!*

"Firework" - Katy Perry

"Hero" - Mariah Carey

I am... *YOUR AFFIRMATION*

I am a firework! I now ignite my light and will shine!

Gosh you have done a lot of work. Good on you!!! I am cheering you on from the sidelines!

Hello Super-Woman!

Are you a parent? Do you ever find yourself saying things that your parents said and cringing because you can't believe you are repeating them?! And yet you find yourself doing it again and again because you don't 'seem' to have any control over the behaviour? So, more and more, you are becoming like your parents?!

If you are not a parent, perhaps you can remember your parents saying things like, 'Oh dear, I sound just like my mum/dad!' Can you recall any behavioural similarities between your grandparents and your parents?!

It may not be all bad by the way. My grandad's nickname for me when I was little was 'Big Fat Lump'! It was said very affectionately - I was far from a fat lump! I call my son a lump now too. He is such a skinny, string bean of a thing and yet lump feels such a loving, affectionate thing to call him. And he knows the energy behind the nickname is purely positive. He also knows my family used to call me a fat lump - the generational links make it really meaningful to him and he loves it.

Such generational links can be really negative though, as we have already learned. And when we habitually and unconsciously copy our parents we are doing it because we still have a cord linking us to them. In order to become an adult who stands healthily separate and unique from our parents we must cut the generational tie. It's as if the umbilical cord has not been severed. It may have been cut physically but energetically we are linked and that is what's holding us back.

You have probably heard it said that energetically we are all one. I believe that to be true and there have been enormous amounts of scientific research done to prove this to be the case. So, although I am talking about our need to energetically cut the cord with our parents, we must remember that we will always be connected energetically. It is our intention behind that connection which is key. Our intention needs to be powered by feelings of compassion, understanding, forgiveness and unconditional love. We can cut the negative connection and replace it with a positive connection. We have a choice. We can keep the good stuff and lose the stuff that makes us feel uncomfortable and not ourselves.

So if everything is energy then would you agree that it makes sense that our thoughts, emotions and feelings are also energy? And if our thoughts, emotions and feelings are energetically created, then they can be energetically released or changed? I would like to invite you to open your mind and consider that this is the truth.

The emotions we have that are uncomfortable, that feel uncontrollable and not 'us', have been adopted emotionally. As a very young child, our intellect had not fully developed so we operated from an emotional state. It was an egocentric survival mode that emotionally took on board our parents' emotional traits. So, in order to energetically release these traits (which, as we became adults, have also become our thoughts and feelings), we need to emotionally release them, thereby freeing the negative thoughts and feelings.

Before we continue - as Daring & Mighty, consciously aware Super Heroes in search of the truth - I want to show you the connectedness of thoughts, emotions and feelings and the difference between an emotion and a feeling. It may just add another dimension to your understanding around how we can energetically cut the cord with our parents.

I love the way the Sanskrit Tradition (the language of Buddhism) explains this. The Sanskrit Tradition defines feelings as the union of thought and emotion. It also says that we are capable of only two primary emotions - love, and whatever the opposite of love is for you. Usually it is said to be fear. So we are either having a love-based emotion or a fear-based emotion. Our emotion is derived from a thought, so our thoughts are either love- or fear-based. Our awareness of the emotion is a feeling.

It is important to identify the difference between an emotion and a feeling because it is only the consciously aware person that can experience or create a feeling. If you are not aware of your emotions, then you are not feeling them. An emotion will dictate a mood you are in. If you often feel 'moody', this is being controlled by an emotion that stemmed from a thought. If you are unconscious, you will be in a mood and probably accept it as 'your lot'. You are a victim to it. A conscious person will notice the mood and question why they are experiencing this emotion. If they are feeling angry, they will ask themselves why. They will go to their thoughts and find the answer. So you could be in an irritable, angry mood. When you become conscious of the anger you feel angry and then you might identify that you are angry because of something someone said to you yesterday that's festered away in your subconscious and become an emotion. Feeling it means you can express it and that is the first step to feeling better. Suddenly you have some control over your emotions and therefore over how you feel.

Daring & Mighty people want to FEEL because we know that to express a feeling about something that is not serving us means we can release it. We are done with being numb. To feel a tough emotion is better than being a victim to it. And we know that experiencing and expressing that tough emotion is what will free us. We dare to decide how we want to feel and can choose love-based thoughts to ensure we feel and project love into every aspect of our mighty lives!

Feelings are the capacity of the heart whereas emotions are linked to brain patterns. In order to feel and embody love, we need to begin to operate from our heart, not our head. When we are operating from our heart, we are able to utilise the powerful healing energy of forgiveness and compassion. This is the gold that will set you free!

But first.....

So far, we have formed an incredible amount of awareness around the negative traits that have controlled you the majority of your life. In every exercise, I asked you to get in touch with your feelings around each awareness. There was a reason for this. I wanted you to build up the energy of anger and frustration around your awareness of every negative trait you have adopted. The more connected you are to the feelings, the greater your experience will be when releasing them - which is what we will begin to do now!

In order to energetically release the stuff that has been holding you back, we are going to get physical! The idea here is to use your body. Whether that means writing, screaming or bashing the crap out of a pillow, you need to physically do something. A specific thought and emotion will be released through the physical activity of your body. We can't *think* ourselves out of this stuff!

Before I did the Hoffman Process, I completed a questionnaire. One of the questions asked was: What are your concerns or fears about doing the Hoffman Process? My answer, word for word, was:

"I am petrified of completely coming undone and being a crumpled, dribbling mess on the floor! I am scared that there is anger, fear and hurt buried so deep that when it is accessed, I will not know how to cope with the emotions. Sometimes, when I really get in touch with my pain, I cry and I get to a point where if I let myself, I could let out a gutteral, animal sound. Sounds odd perhaps, but I feel there is this 'noise' inside of me that needs to come out and I have never felt confident enough or able to go there. I am embarrassed and self-conscious, even on my own. So I am scared this might come up and I will have to 'make the noise'!"

As much as anger can be a wonderfully motivating force (it is partly why you are reading this book!), in our society it is rare to be taught how to express anger - which is so sad, because it can be such a putrid and destructive emotion when left to fester. We are taught to rationalise our emotions because God forbid you be 'emotional'! Being emotional has been bandied about as a negative thing. We tell our children not to be so 'dramatic' when they express their emotions. I was told to 'be quiet and stop being so difficult!' My expression of my emotions was too much for my parents - they could barely contend with their own emotions, let alone mine. They were hell bent on suppressing and covering up their emotions. Witnessing me as a young girl and worse, as a teenage girl, attempting to express my anger probably alerted them to their own uncomfortable feelings. Far better to mute us all!

The thing is, we can't rationalise our emotions. Our rational mind and our brain can't control our emotions. Once they are out there, they are out there! We can start to alter our thought patterns which, in turn, mean healthier emotions, but if we have been living with unhealthy thought patterns for a long time, the emotions are going to come on thick and strong. If we choose to ignore or repress them (therefore, not 'feel' them), they are going to bite us on the bum when we least expect it and that makes us feel totally out of control. It's horrible.

They say that depression is long term repression. Does that ring true for you? It certainly does for me. You see, if you are suppressing your anger and frustration, then you are also suppressing your joy and happiness.

When I wrote about making 'the noise', I was getting in touch with an intuition that was telling me I had repressed anger for so long it had festered and almost literally become like a caged, feral animal. I had no experience or guidance throughout my life on how to healthily release my anger as it came up. I was embarrassed and self-conscious at the idea of even admitting to the anger inside me, let alone expressing it. But my experience is not unique to me. Do you feel anger inside you that needs to come out? I bet after all the exercises we have done, you have bucket loads. Go get your boxing gloves, girl, it's time to release that inner tiger!

 *PUMP UP THE VOLUME!*

"Eye Of The Tiger" - Survivor (Rocky IV Soundtrack)

I am... *YOUR AFFIRMATION*

It is safe for me to express all of my emotions.

 *AN EXERCISE*

There are many ways to express anger, and I am going to give you a few ideas here. No doubt you will have heard many of them before but perhaps have felt too embarrassed or uncomfortable or guilty to do them. Please do yourself a favour and let all of that go! Haven't you been holding onto your discomfort and anger for long enough? There is no need to feel guilty; no one but you knows you are doing these exercises. You are putting yourself first because you value yourself enough to be set free of all that is holding you back. What is the point of feeling embarrassed and uncomfortable? Don't you feel more embarrassed and uncomfortable when you are acting out in ways that do not serve you? When you are throwing tantrums in front of your partner? Or unreasonably screaming at your kids? Or losing the plot when a waiter gets your order wrong?!

1. DANCE! This is a fab one. Dance it out. Put on some music that really gets you pumped. No Michael Bolton or Barbara Streisand, please! I'm thinking Rage Against The Machine, Pearl Jam, Wolf Mother. Or what about some serious Drum 'n' Bass? Or some Rock and Hip Hop? Anything that gets you moving and allows you to stamp your feet and throw yourself about the room!! You know that wonderful saying: 'Dance as if no one is watching!' Well, NO ONE is watching. Go nuts. Close the curtains and hurl yourself about the living room floor. Focus on a single fear-based thought or negative trait that you are FED UP with. DECIDE that you want to be free of it. Set the intention that you will hip-hop your heart out until you feel the intensity of the emotion connected to your feelings around that trait dissipate. It could take more than one dance session, depending on the intensity of the feelings and how deeply ingrained they are. Tune in and feel where you are at with it. After just one good foot thumping session, I bet you will feel better. Not least because you are giving yourself permission to express your feelings and you are saying to the Universe, in no uncertain terms, that you are absolutely done with feeling this way and intend to replace these feelings and thoughts with loving, happy, nurturing, joyful and creative ones!

2. RUN! If you are a runner, imagine the fearful thought or uncomfortable behaviour is on the bottom of your shoe. If you have two traits that are quite similar or seem to tie together for you – such as 'fault finder' and 'blamer' – put one underneath each shoe. Imagine the word or the circumstances around each word are firmly glued to the base of each shoe and then run the crap out of them. Beat the pavement with them. With every step you take, imagine that you are crushing the life out of it. As with the dancing, set your intention, decide what you want to let go of and kill off those things as you run. Play some angry tunes in your headphones as you do it to really fire you up!

3. SWIM! If you are a swimmer, put the named traits on the body part that's thrashing the water. So if you are doing a kicking action, put them on your feet (don't forget we are being imaginary! We don't want people at your local pool thinking you are unhinged. We are going more for Daring & Mighty!). If you are doing butterfly, whack them on your hands. Every time your feet or hands hit the water, imagine you are thumping the life out of the trait.

4. WRITE! As you have already discovered, writing is a fabulous tool. Hand-write exhaustively about why you are so fed up with a particular trait. Yell and scream and swear – in writing. Scribble out your anger. Call people who have done this to you all the nasty names under the sun. Use thick black marker pen to really see the putrid darkness of your anger. Then burn it. You do not need the negative energy of this writing in your life anymore. Burn it and know that as it burns, so do the traits. They are now ashes. And, like a phoenix rising from the ashes, you are reborn! Celebrate your freedom as you watch the flames engulf all your hatred thoughts. This is such a liberating exercise and it's so important you let all your emotions surface and that you feel the release and excitement for the new future awaiting you. A future which is now in your control!

5. BASH! This is a tool that Hoffman uses when you experience their process in person -which I highly recommend! There are a few companies now that offer safe environments allowing you to bash out your anger, so if you don't want to do this alone, you can join the high energy of a group of people bashing the crap out of a pillow! I love 'The Tantrum Club' for the way they apply this work. The idea here is to get a bat or a rolling pin or even just your fists. Then imagine the named trait is sitting on the pillow in front of you - and pulverize it. Yell and scream while you do it. Similar to the writing exercise, express your anger. Say why you are angry. Say what you are not willing to put up with any more. Cry. Shout. Make 'the noise'. I can't tell you how liberating this is. And, as with all methods, gauge how you are feeling at the end. If you think you haven't quite killed the trait, plan another session. Perhaps try another method. Keep at it until you feel, in your gut, you have let go of that behavioural pattern or fear.

Preparation is key! If you plan and prepare to do any of these exercises then you can ensure you are doing it in a safe environment that makes you feel comfortable and secure. If that means joining a group who are expressing anger, do that. Planning also means you are in control - you are not just having a tantrum. You are setting an intention.

Remember, the Universe is going to support you on this journey. As I said before, you are setting an intention and saying to the Universe that you are ready to let this stuff go and start to create a life you love. Believe me, a power so much greater than you will support you in this decision. I promise!

So, Daring & Mighty Superwoman, this brings us to the end of Part 1!

CONGRATULATIONS!

Do you feel as if you have given your 100% energy to figuring out where you are at in your life - Right Here, Right Now - and why? Remember, no one can do this work except you. This stuff takes persistence and dogged determination. Let your REASON WHY motivate you and your VISION for your future pull you forward. Focus on that end goal. The gorgeous, shining, joyful person you know you really are is waiting for you. She is there, she is free and she is bloody excited for you. So am I!

You now have the first tool to start to release some of the stuff that has been holding you back. Enjoy the liberation of expressing your anger. Really go for it!

In Part 2 you are going to connect to your Spirit and your heart and ask that they help you to release all that has been holding you back. So get your meditation space ready because we will be doing some lovely healing and connecting meditations. Your Self-Love Affair is about to begin! I hope you're pumped! Let's celebrate all your hard work so far......

 *PUMP UP THE VOLUME!*

"Celebration" - Kylie Minogue

I am... *YOUR AFFIRMATION*

I am Daring & Mighty. I am in control of how I feel. I am creating a life I love!

PART 2: MY SPIRIT. MY TRUTH.

Just before sitting down to write this section, I was having a meeting with my producer about some videos we are creating for my website. On the spur of the moment, I decided to show him some videos that I recorded a few years ago but had never shared. They are incredibly raw accounts of exactly how I was feeling at the time and how passionately determined I was to help other women who had experienced themselves and their lives in a similar way to me. I wanted to make it easier for them to find help that would create deep and profound change in their lives. I was so moved to be reminded of where I was and how I felt. At that time, although I had shifted a lot of 'stuff' and was well and truly on the Daring & Mighty path, I still had some tough stuff to clear. As a single parent with a just-three-year-old in tow, that was one mighty challenge. I watched footage of me sharing lessons around 'Persistence' and 'Determination' while on a camping trip with my son, who piped up in the background and started singing *"I'm on my way from misery to happiness today, ah ha ah ha ah ha ah ha!"* You know that Proclaimers song?! It was on the 'Shrek' soundtrack and it was his song of the moment. I burst into tears as I watched the footage of that gorgeous, innocent little boy singing away. I was reminded of the bravery and determination I had mustered at that point to really take my life to another level. I had left a relationship; I had nowhere to live, no savings, no car and no job. But I had hope! And a seed of an idea around how I could help others. I also had a small child depending on me. That was when my Self-Love Affair really began and I started to develop a very deep connection with my Spirit and a profound trust in a Universal power that was holding me. I experienced a profound spiritual awakening that took my life to another level. Fast forward just a handful of years and I have never felt stronger or happier. My home is a beautiful little cottage in the Sussex countryside. I have some money in the bank! I have a car (she is a little beaten up but I love her!). I get to travel a lot. And I don't just have a job - I have a life purpose I love and people pay me for what I do. What a trip! I can't begin to express how proud I feel when my son says to me, 'Mummy, you love yourself, don't you!'

I so desire for YOU to love yourself. I desire that you know your Spirit. I desire that you experience the loving support of the Universe. And that is what we are going to do now. It's time to connect with your Spirit and your heart - they are your truth. They are the power inside you that will enable you to forgive when you thought forgiveness was impossible. To laugh in the face of fear. To feel joyfully certain in your uncertainty. To feel deeply fulfilled with a determination to serve others in a way that is a reflection of your truth.

Let's enjoy that wonderful Proclaimers song and then get to work!

PUMP UP THE VOLUME!

"I'm On My Way" - The Proclaimers

The Truth of You

"I'm here. I love you. I don't care if you need to stay up crying all night long, I will stay with you. There's nothing you can ever do to lose my love. I will protect you until you die, and after your death I will still protect you. I am stronger than Depression and I am braver than Loneliness and nothing will ever exhaust me." Elizabeth Gilbert, 'Eat, Pray, Love'

The discovery of your true Spirit and learning to be guided by that voice is your ticket to living a deeply fulfilled life. Your Spirit IS your Truth.

So what is your Spirit? For me it is a feeling, a sense, an intuition of something inside me that is pure, wise and peaceful. It is unaffected by my negative experiences and judgements – it remains pure. It is awakened and all-knowing so it has all the answers to my deepest truths. It is pure love. It is my Soul, my Higher Self, my Inner Guide, my Voice, my Essence. It has always been with me. It is me. And it is the best possible version of me! So when I wake up in the morning, I ask my Spirit to guide me, ensuring I operate throughout the day to my highest will and good. For Daring & Mighty peeps, it's the only way to roll!

I bet if you have read this far, you have a strong sense that you have something pure and wise within you. Am I right? Perhaps you already feel a connection to 'you'? Why not decide now to deepen that connection. Are you up for it? If you want your life to become miraculous, your connection to your higher self is crucial. It is where all your answers are. If you are constantly asking, 'What is my purpose?', 'What am I meant to do with my life?!', 'What is the answer to X?', 'How can I heal Y?" – you need to tune into your Spirit for your answers. No one can do this for you and your answers have to come from you. This is *your* life – no one else's.

 *A MEDITATION*

The True-Self Visualisation - you can download the audio of this meditation for free at: http://daringandmighty.com/meditation-library

Prepare your meditation space, light a candle and enjoy this beautiful 15-minute visualisation.

This is something you can do every day.

Even if you only spend five minutes when you wake up to simply breath and connect with yourself, it will make such a big difference, setting up your day nicely with that all-important intention that you desire to be guided by your True Self.

When I started to meditate and develop a connection with my Spirit, people around me really noticed. They would comment that I was calmer, more open and more approachable. People that had never met me presumed I had always been this way and labelled me as a bit of a hippy. They liked my calm, warm energy. I haven't always been that way! It still surprises me when people say they enjoy my calmness. It makes me laugh because most of my life I have been a bundle of anxiety and worry!

Guided visualisations and meditations are incredibly powerful tools that also allow you to completely stop and unwind. There are many ways you can connect to your Spirit. Meditation is just one and you may find your own way. You might just like to chat with yourself! Perhaps journalling helps you to hear the voice of your Spirit. Painting or being creative can connect you internally. Taking a walk or run in nature, yoga, dancing or swimming can help you to connect. It's important to find whatever works for you. Perhaps it will be more than one thing. I love a mix of meditation, journalling, painting and walking. It's all about being calm, comfortable and peacefully lost (and yet found!) within yourself. It's gorgeous!

A spiritual awakening can come in many forms. For some it's an instant and profound experience, especially if it comes on the back of a life or death situation. We hear more and more near death accounts of people experiencing themselves as a Spirit in physical form and of 'the light' beyond. I have met people who have recovered from depression with suicidal thoughts to experience profound spiritual awareness because they came so close to taking their own life. They were given a reason to keep going - to discover their purpose and make that their gift to the world. Something was telling them they hadn't completed their mission yet! For some it is a slower process. There is usually an openness or willingness to connect to something deeper followed by synchronicities that offer proof of a Spirit world and guidance towards ways of connection that will best suit them. When you start to identify what your 'thing' is, you will very naturally want to do more of it because it feels so great to be in connection - whether it's running, music or meditation.

My spiritual awakening was a slow drip. I always knew in my heart that there was something bigger than me. I just couldn't put my finger on it. I started off very traditionally with church youth groups as a teenager. I enjoyed some elements of that. I didn't enjoy being repeatedly told I was a sinner though and after a few bad experiences with some church leaders, I rebelled and moved as far away from that environment as I could possibly get. The thing is, during my experience of Christianity and the church, I did meet some fabulous people who really walked their talk and seemed to be full of light and love. I also had experiences of profound love and knew there was a God in some form. For me, that love wasn't meant to have walls built around it in the form of a church. Although I managed to push down and ignore 'God' for quite a few years, it was always inside me. I always knew there was something special within and around me and when times got tough, I would call out to that power and ask for help. If I ever found myself in a church, I always enjoyed the calm energy and I often sensed something special in those spaces. Slowly I recovered from the fear-based teachings around God and started to experience this power in ways that spoke to me. I came to call that power 'the Light' and 'the Universe' because those terms sat more comfortably with me. My openness was then met with messages from my mum, who had passed away many years earlier, via unexpected people. I experienced hypnotherapy and guided visualisations with a life coach, which opened my awareness more deeply to Spirit. I learned meditation techniques that had profound effects – not just in terms of spiritual connection but in creating massive shifts in my thought processes and belief systems. I met various spiritual teachers who introduced me to my Spirit Guides and Angels and I developed an unwavering faith that I had a Spiritual Team working with me at all times. I often call on my 'team' to help me when I need it! Whenever I was 'ready' to go to the next level, I was guided to read, watch, hear or meet that someone who would show me the way. Willingness to explore was the key and now there is no looking back! I can't imagine my world without this awareness and every person I have ever spoken to who has had a spiritual awakening of some form says the same. The Truth will set you free, as they say!

As you begin to cut through all the layers that have covered your Spirit for so long, you will start to hear her voice and know her divine purpose. As you develop this relationship, you will begin to develop faith in this power and trust that she can help you to forgive, heal and move forward. She can help you to create the life you have been dreaming of. You will not be able to help but fall in love with her. To love yourself will be inevitable and what a gift! Ooh, I feel a song coming on! It's time to hand over to Whitney....

PUMP UP THE VOLUME!

"Greatest Love of All" - Whitney Houston

I am... **YOUR AFFIRMATION**

My Spirit is my Truth. I trust her to guide me every day, to my highest will and good.

Lighten the Load

"When you hold resentment toward another, you are bound to that person or condition by an emotional link that is stronger than steel. Forgiveness is the only way to dissolve that link and get free." Catherine Ponder

Forgiveness happens at a soul level. When we learn to connect to our Spirit, we can heal all hurt, fear, injustice and wrongdoing. We do not need to know 'how' to forgive. The key is surrendering to that power inside us that knows us best and trusting that it will show us the way free.

I understood forgiveness on an intellectual level for a long time. The thing with forgiveness is that you need to actually experience it to really get it. That means you need to get on and do it. You can read all the books you like. This stuff can't be sorted out in your mind. You must take action and trust that your Spirit always has your highest will and good at heart.

It is easy to think that you need to wait to be 'ready' to forgive and in some cases, I can understand that a little time may need to elapse before you can do this work. However, most of us hold onto resentments for far too long and the only person that is hurting as a result is us. Buddha said that to not forgive is like picking up a hot coal with the intention of throwing it at the person we are angry with but as we hold that coal the person that gets most burned is us. When you hold onto resentful, vengeful thoughts, it is you that is being hurt. Not the person you perceive to have wronged you.

Think about how you feel when you are remembering the hurt someone caused you in the past. No doubt you feel hot with anger, your chest and throat are probably constricted, you 'see black' and you feel uncomfortable, moody and far from at ease. Your energy is contracting. Holding onto thoughts and feelings like this causes dis-ease. Only you are being hurt and probably getting sick. The person that 'wronged' you doesn't feel a thing! The longer you hold onto this stuff, the more damage you are doing to yourself. And the longer you are thinking thoughts of injustice and wrongdoing, the more you are attracting experiences of injustice and wrongdoing into your life. We will look at the laws around attraction in Part 3. For now, please trust this to be the truth.

Every time you feel anger towards someone, you are remembering a situation that caused you pain so are re-living that moment over and over again. Why do that to yourself?

Please know that every thought you have either darkens or lightens your world. Why not choose to let go of the dark thoughts? The way to do this is to forgive. Forgive the thought, forgive yourself for having the thought and forgive the person the thought is directed towards. All you need do is set an 'intention'. There is that word again!

We have already learned that you are a Spirit in a body and that your Spirit's 'job' is to evolve and grow. I wonder if you have opened your mind to the earlier suggestion that your Spirit chose the family you were born into so you would be given perfect opportunities for growth? That said, could you stretch your mind to believing that the negative traits you have adopted from your parents placed you in situations which, if your perception would allow, were an opportunity for growth? They say we learn from our mistakes. Well, we do if we choose to perceive the error as a lesson and then decide not to do it again. If we choose to try a different way, then we are learning from our mistakes. It is all about perception and choice. Could you stretch your mind again to consider that all the tough stuff you experienced and adopted from your parents was actually a gift? This is what I believe having experienced deep forgiveness for both my parents. I can now see with absolute clarity that my lessons have enabled me to start living a life that feels truly free and deeply me. If you can start to believe that the 'stuff' you want to overcome is, on a soul level, gifts from the Spirits of your parents or surrogates, could that make the forgiving process easier for you? You see, it is our perception that will block our ability to forgive or not.

"Forgiveness is a shift in perception that removes a block in me to my awareness of love's presence." A Course in Miracles

Before we started looking at your childhood programming, we looked at the idea that love is the driving force behind everything. Do you remember? That it is our essence and what connects us, internally and externally? With that in mind, I would like to share with you another teaching from 'A Course in Miracles', which says:

"Every act is either an expression of love or a call for love, regardless of how unskillful it may appear."

If you can stretch your mind to believe that everything that happens is an act of love, it is easier to have compassion towards someone's behaviour and that is the first step towards forgiveness. You see, if you could consider that when someone seemingly wrongs you they are offering you a gift of love - a gift of growth and therefore the evolution of your Spirit - then you are taking the negative charge away from the situation. You suddenly have no reason at all to be mad. There isn't even anything to forgive. In fact, if you do have a moment of resentful thinking, you may want to forgive yourself for, in that moment, you have moved away from love and towards its opposite - fear. The only way back to love is through forgiveness.

I love the Hawaiian Mantra, 'Ho'ponopono':

> *Dear Father*
>
> *I am sorry*
>
> *Please forgive me*
>
> *I love you*
>
> *Thank you*

My understanding of this prayer is that you are acknowledging a power greater than us, that is, unconditional love. We say sorry for having forgotten its gift of love in all things and offer up love and gratitude to return us to a state of pure love.

I have used this mantra when I am acknowledging that I made a decision to perceive a 'gift' from a person as a 'wrongdoing'. My intention is to forgive myself and ask forgiveness from the 'gift' giver - on a soul level - for choosing fear over love, thereby returning us both back to a state of love. I have experienced profound healing by chanting the Ho'ponopono repeatedly. Again, it is a mental leap; however, when you sit in meditation and allow your Spirit to work through you, these words take on an energy that is quite remarkable to witness.

With compassion, you can start to understand why your parents behaved the way they did. In the same way that you have taken on their negative traits unconsciously as an egocentric child, so too did your parents take on their traits from their parents. They are only operating in the way they were shown. If they were consciously aware, they would have been able to connect with the uncomfortable feelings and behavioural patterns that did not serve them and they would have had the choice, as you do, to do something about it. You are in the fabulous position of benefitting from the teachings of incredibly gifted and intuitive psychotherapists and psychiatrists. We now live in a generation that has access to this kind of material, helping us to develop compassion for our parents and ourselves. I think it's so liberating too that we have moved away from a culture of blame to one of accepting responsibility for our own lives. Blaming Mum and Dad for stuff is so outdated. It's time for a new way of being - a time for self-responsibility and if we choose to have children, choosing to consciously parent.

Remember how we learned that we need to stand separate from our parents to be truly free? That we need to cut the emotional ties with them? We have begun to cut those ties through physical energetic release and I hope you are continuing your practices of expression in ways that work for you. Now we need to do it through forgiveness -

another emotional release. As Catherine Ponder said above, *'Forgiveness is the only way to dissolve that link and get free.'*

With compassion for our parents and surrogates as egocentric children, let's forgive them.

With compassion, we can also forgive ourselves for treating ourselves and others in a less than loving way.

There is no blame. No fault. Forgiveness will simply set us all free.

Hand over control to your Spirit and its infinite capacity for forgiveness and unconditional love.

 *AN EXERCISE*

Please do be kind to yourself as you enter into these exercises for forgiveness. Do not put it off though. And remember that forgiveness may not happen overnight, but it will happen and you will know about it! Just keep at it.

Here are a few writing exercises for you. Do them as and when you feel comfortable, over a period of time. You need to allow yourself time and space for this work because it is so important that it is a deeply emotional experience. You need to connect with all the uncomfortable, angry, resentful and regretful feelings so you can truly forgive and be set free.

Forgiving Parents / Surrogates

Choose a pattern or memory that is the focus of your forgiveness. Write a letter to your Spirit, asking for help to forgive your parents and surrogates. If relevant, ask that you also be forgiven for the role you may have played. Get really honest and write all your thoughts and feelings around the pattern and/or memory. As much as we have identified above that the tough lessons were gifts of love, you will still very rightly have a lot of emotions that need to be acknowledged right now. Even if your parents didn't mean to hurt you and even if they were playing a role in the evolution of your soul, you have still experienced a lot of pain and that needs to be expressed in this letter. Your pain is very real and with forgiveness, you can let it go. When you have written about your experiences and pain, start to imagine what life must have been like for your parents / surrogates as children. Start to express your compassion for their life as a dependent child because you know that as an adult, they still carry the pain and discomfort of that small child. That they are an expression of that child. Imagine how they must have felt when they were small. Ask your Spirit to help you to see past all the pain and ask that you see the truth of your parents. Ask that you witness the purity of their Spirits. Whether your parents are alive or dead, on a soul level you can ask to connect to their Spirits and offer them peace, love and forgiveness. Ask that you also be forgiven if you know in your heart that you played a role too. When you feel as if all you need to express is on paper, write: *I forgive you and I set you free. I forgive us both and I set myself free.*

Forgiving Yourself

Choose a mistake or memory or negative chatter that is the focus of your forgiveness. Write a letter to your Spirit, asking for help to forgive yourself. Write about the nasty things you have said to yourself and the self-inflicted pain you have caused. Write about the pain you have caused others. Write about behaviours and actions you regret. Set a clear intention that you are ready to let it all go and start a fresh. That you will be kind to yourself and others because with compassion, you can see that your mistakes are forgivable and your negative chatter is not your truth. As you deepen the connection with your Spirit, offer yourself peace, love and forgiveness. Ask that you be connected to the Spirit of the person(s) you have wronged and that, on a soul level, they experience your offering of love and healing. When you feel as if all you need to express is on paper, write: *I forgive myself and I set myself free. I forgive myself and I love myself unconditionally.*

After writing a letter, go to your meditation space and light a candle.

 *A MEDITATION*

The Forgiveness Meditation – you can download the audio of this meditation for free at: http://daringandmighty.com/meditation-library

Prepare your meditation space, light a candle, sit with your letter in your lap and enjoy this beautiful 15-minute visualisation.

When you complete the meditation, burn the letter and know that you have been set free.

If you feel as if you want to write about your experience of forgiveness after the meditation, do so. It will allow you to really connect with the wonderfully liberating feeling of forgiveness. Enjoy the freedom. Feel the release!

When you feel deeply that you have forgiven yourself, your parents / surrogates and anyone else you identified, you may want to express your love and forgiveness in person. If you feel safe and able to do so, why not tell these people that you love them? Ask those you have wronged for their forgiveness in person. You have done this work on a soul level but we are physical beings too and expressing love and forgiveness in person deepens and shares the experience. The key thing is not to expect anything in return. In fact, you may be met with upset or anger. Stay in your power, express your love and leave it at that. Go with the intention of offering your love and vulnerability without expectation. Ask for forgiveness without expectation. You will need to feel very safe to do this work in person so set it up with that in mind.

 *A MEDITATION*

"Ra Ma Da Sa" - available on the Spotify Playlist: http://spoti.fi/1H0Gvz0

Ra Ma Da Sa Sa Say So Hung is one of the most powerful mantras known and is used for healing in the mental, spiritual, emotional and physical levels. This mantra connects you with the pure healing energy of the Universe and the words literally mean, 'I am Thou' – the service of God is within me.

I think it is a lovely meditation to do when you have gone through an exercise on forgiveness. It is also very healing if you feel anxious, fearful or worried. It helps you to centre and connect with your Spirit and the Universe.

Light a candle and sit up straight with your legs crossed. Your eyes are closed and focused toward your third eye (middle of your forehead). Bend your arms and bring the elbows against the side of the rib cage. Your forearms move out to the side and your palms are open and facing upwards (as if you are a waitress holding a plate on each side of your body). Your elbows remain touching your sides. As you sing the mantra, imagine the person you are forgiving (or yourself) is bathed in healing white light. Every time you breathe in, know that healing and forgiveness is being sent to that person (or to you).

 *PUMP UP THE VOLUME!*

"Ra Ma Da Sa" - Snatam Kaur

"Long Time Sun" - Snatam Kaur

I am... YOUR AFFIRMATIONS

I forgive you and I set you free.

I forgive myself and I set myself free.

I forgive myself and I love myself unconditionally.

I am available for miracles.

Dear Father; I am sorry; Please forgive me; I love you; Thank you. ('Ho'ponopono')

The Child Inside

Ok, Daring & Mighty Super Hero!! It's time to get comfortable with the idea of loving yourself.

Do you Dare to love your Mighty self?! Do you feel as if your Self-Love Affair has begun? Or are you still wincing at the thought?

I hope you are coming around to the idea that you are pretty effing fabulous by now! You have been digging deep and can see that much of what has been holding you back has been 'False Evidence Appearing Real', programmed belief and behavioural systems of others, resentments and anger. You have started to clear away this muck and are slowly uncovering your beautiful truth. Would you agree? Yes? Go on, say YES!

You are now starting to perceive all your lessons as beautiful gifts. These gifts have been cracking you open to reveal the true you and those cracks have allowed the light in, to shine on your Truth. The Truth that you are pure love. That love will start to seep out, filling and fulfilling you and when you are full up, it will flow to others with such ease and warmth. You will develop the ability to have healthy boundaries and to receive love from others simultaneously. I am so excited for you!

Loving yourself is absolutely about falling in love with your Spirit - the real you. I believe it is also about developing a relationship with your inner child. Whoa, hold on! What?! First I ask you to discover your Spirit inside, and now I'm telling you that you have a small child in there too?! What next...?! Don't worry, there is no one else there (that I know of!). Your child *does* need a lot of love though so it's important we pay her some attention now.

When you were doing the forgiveness writing exercise, you may remember you were asked to express your compassion for your parents / carers as dependent children because you know that as an adult, they still carry the pain and discomfort of that small child. Same goes for you. As an adult, you are emotionally holding onto the feelings of you as a little girl. It is a very real energy inside you. Have you heard it said that emotions are Energy in Motion - E-Motion? Well, the energy of your childhood emotions is still with you and it can feel as if you literally do have a small child inside you. Usually we only notice her when she is screaming for our attention! That is when we tend to tantrum and rage like a child, express 'neediness' and search for someone to 'parent' and nurture us. When we have children of our own, those buttons get pressed so quickly if we haven't learned to pay our child inside the attention she deserves. When we love and honour the child within us, we are much more able to serve our children at our best, for their best - with patience and understanding. We are also able to have friendships and intimate partnerships that are not about fulfilling the neediness. We stop looking for a parental figure to nurture us because we know how to nurture ourselves.

If you think back to the work we did around how you inherited your parents' negative patterns, do you remember how we identified that you took those on emotionally, because your intellect hadn't fully developed yet? It is the energy of your small child that holds onto all that negative stuff. Fear, anxiety and shame - whatever was your experience as a child - is what defines your inner child now. It's not all negative though. Your inner child is also playful, curious, joyful, free, spontaneous, funny, cheeky and perfectly crazy! You are a blend of all sorts of characteristics - positive and negative. Loving yourself is all about unconditionally accepting and understanding them all. We need to listen to the voice of our inner child. To hear her when she is feeling alone, unloveable, worried, insecure, too much, not enough or unsafe. If she knows she is being heard and if we can offer her love and understanding, she will feel empowered to express her joy and playfulness. And we need fun in our lives!!

At this point, I think it's important to be really clear that you didn't pick up conditioning or programming that isn't serving you from just your parents or immediate carers. Indeed, no doubt when you were doing your expression and forgiveness work, other people came up that you know have had an impact on your life. It's likely that the other people impacted your life beyond the formative early stages and yet they still imparted messaging around the idea that love is conditional. Remember, when you arrived into the world you were whole and you were pure love. As you grew up, depending on the people that had influence on your life, you either learned to embrace that truth or to move away from it in varying degrees. So siblings, relatives, teachers, friends, godparents, baby-sitters, housekeepers....they all modelled to you in some way what love is, and more than likely, the messages you learned were that love is conditional. In fact, beyond the people closest to you, you were also shown how to love, be loved and experience yourself as love by all sorts of external factors, from Madonna to The Beatles, from 'The Brady Bunch' to 'ET', from Cosmo Magazine to Enid Blyton, from Barbie to Ken!

We learn how to behave, what to say, how to look and so forth by interpreting the variety of messages we get from a whole host of sources around what equals love. We subconsciously ask ourselves, "Who do I need to be to be loved?" We lose sight of our truth - that we are more than enough just as we are.

To use myself as an example, as an adult I have had to tackle big beliefs about myself that stem from all sorts of messages I received from family, friends, society and the media.

I am not sexy

I am not pretty

I am not intelligent

I am annoying

I am too emotional

I am too needy

I am not thoughtful

I am too smart

I am too giggly

I am not happy

I am not helpful

I am not a nice person

I am selfish

I am always sick

I am annoying

I am not clever

I am too noisy

I am shy

I am a show-off

I could go on, but I think you get the idea! I wonder if you can relate to any of these?

All of these pretty much boil down to two distinct beliefs:

I am not enough

I am too much

In his book, "Loveability", Robert Holden writes how he believes our basic fear is 'I am not loveable'. He says, "*...it feeds our negative self-concepts. It shows us an unloveable self-image. It convinces us to abandon our authentic nature and to adopt a role that will hopefully save us from more rejection.*"

Robert goes on to write about the idea that the beliefs, 'I am not enough' and 'I am too much', feed directly into the 'basic fear' that 'I am not loveable'. It's at the root of all fears.

Pretty full-on, huh!

Reading back over the list of beliefs above, would you agree they sound rather childish!? As real and as horrible as some of them have felt in my life, to my mind they do have a childish ring to them. Almost whingy! It's because I took those beliefs on emotionally and my emotional age spanned the majority of my pre-teens. So I have been attempting to operate in adulthood and have healthy intimate relationships with a small child running the show!

Despite clearing out some enormous limiting beliefs and behaviours and absolutely stepping into my adult self, standing securely separate from my parents, my inner child still battles with some varieties of the fear that 'I am not loveable'. My inner 'good girl' is sometimes still desperate to be loved and wants to please everyone else in order to get it. My inner 'clever girl' sometimes still craves approval. My inner 'sick girl' occasionally comes up for attention, thinking that being ill is the only way to secure love or approval.

Paying my inner child attention allows me to step into the role of mature adult and offer unconditional love to that child. It's not too late! Connecting with my inner child allows me to heal old wounds on another level. It allows me to feel nurtured and safe without the need to seek it from others. I am better able to manage my seven-year-old when he is playing up because my inner child is heard and understood. The way I relate to friends and colleagues is less childish as a result of caring for my little girl within.

So, my friend, it's time to embrace your inner child. She is a very real part of you and self-love is all about accepting - with unconditional love, understanding and compassion - all parts of you.

You have welcomed in your Spirit. Now it's time to welcome in your Little Girl!

AN EXERCISE

Let's start to develop your relationship with your inner child. In the same way that you have started to connect with and talk to your Spirit, start to form a bond of understanding and presence with your Little Girl inside.

As you go about your day-to-day life today, consider that you are an adult, nurturing a child. All day long, keep an awareness within that you are taking care of your special little girl all day. Let her know that you intend to hang out with her today. That you want to get to know her. Let her know that you will listen to her. Notice her. Comfort her when she is worried or frightened. Give her permission to play and dream when she feels like it. Set an alarm on your phone every couple of hours to remind you to check in with your inner child. Don't forget her! This is crucial. Make a vow to yourself that you will pay her attention all day.

If she is raging or sad, sit down and write out those thoughts and feelings. When you feel finished, write: *I have heard you and I understand. From now on I promise to listen to you. I love you and you are safe.*

This may feel a little odd to start with, but as you develop a relationship with your inner child you will begin to see that she is a very real energy within you. As your relationship with that voice develops, she will calm down. She will start to feel safe and chilled out! Her playfulness will emerge! Your role then is to encourage her joyfulness. Give her permission to laugh and skip and dance and tell silly jokes. If you have your own children, use this new energy to play with them. Do cartwheels in the garden! Chew bubblegum and blow massive bubbles together! Get the paints out and make a mess! Kids love mess, and your inner child will go nuts! Enjoy it.

 *A MEDITATION*

Connecting With Your Inner Child Meditation – you can download the audio of this meditation for free at: http://daringandmighty.com/meditation-library

Prepare your meditation space, light a candle and enjoy this beautiful 15-minute visualisation whenever you desire to be in deeper connection with your inner child.

I am... *YOUR AFFIRMATIONS*

I accept my inner child as a very real part of me.

I pay her attention and honour her with unconditional love, understanding and compassion.

 *PUMP UP THE VOLUME*

"Where Do The Children Play?" - Cat Stevens

"My Favourite Things" - Julie Andrews

"Peter & The Wolf" - Sergei Prokofiev

Your S-Team!

As you know, you are a Spirit in a body and your Spirit's mission is to evolve and grow. You are essentially hard-wired to expand. Your Spirit knows no boundaries to expansion. It is limitless. So, just when you think you have overcome your biggest hurdle and stepped into a bigger, more authentic you, it will not be long before you start to feel that familiar pull to want to do it again. It is your operating system!

Us humans tend to think we have to do it all on our own. In fact, we 'think' too much! I am hoping you are far enough into this book now to see the truth in the idea that as energetic beings, we are doing ourselves a far greater service to start to feel more. To feel our way through life. Through the challenges. Indeed, to give ourselves permission to enjoy the highs too!

To tune into your feelings means you are tuning into your intuition too. You are working a muscle that allows you to sense life on a different level - not just from a place of what you can see, hear, touch, taste and physically feel. You can begin to do life in the way that you are most naturally hard-wired to do it. You simply have not grown up in a society that models much more than using your five basic physical senses and attempts to think its way through everything. How's that been working out for you....?!?

Choosing the Daring & Mighty path means choosing to tune into yourself as a spiritual, energetic being of pure love. Sure, your physical, human form serves you well and will continue to do so. You are human, after all! Your human form allows you to experience YOU in a way that you can't when you are just a big loveable bundle of source energy! Your body is your vehicle to knowing yourself better and it allows you to interact with the earth and others in a way that challenges you deeply - giving you opportunity after opportunity to learn from life's obstacles and step ever more deeply into the truth that you are ever expanding love.

So going back to the idea that you think you have to do this alone. Here's the really great news. You don't!

As a Spirit, you have a Spiritual Team who is supporting you on your mission, 24-7. You are not alone.

Here's how I see it. I have the light of God holding me. A gang of Spirit Guides directing and advising me. A group of Angels healing and protecting me. I don't need to do this Daring & Mighty work alone. In fact, I would not be honouring my Spirit if I tried! My Spirit is hooked up with a mighty team that loves me unconditionally and is right behind me, every step of the way.

So I call on whoever I need, when I need them. I know they always have my back.

I feel part of all and all feels part of me. There is no separation in my mind - I simply call forth members of my S-Team to support me when I need it, knowing also that they are ever present, ever on my side, even when I forget to ask for their help. They are there. Always. They are love. Always. And so am I.

Knowing this - actually, more than knowing it; feeling this as my absolute non-negotiable truth - fills me with such security. You may argue that I must be weak in some way. That if I need to believe in this stuff, which is paramount to believing in a Disney fairytale, I am not strong enough in terms of my self-belief, self-trust or self-love. The thing is, when I woke up a few years ago to discover that I am a Spiritual Being - essentially, I had a spiritual awakening - something happened to me that I simply cannot put into words. I woke up to the truth and I experienced life in a profoundly different way. I can't explain it except to say that my eyes were opened and my true sense - my intuition - was suddenly on high alert and I discovered so much loving guidance around me. I was humbled. And I realised that I was weak to have ignored the truth of me and the truth of this almighty team that was desperate to support me. Choosing to do life as we are meant to, as Spiritual Beings, was no simple thing. And yet it was.

Let me explain.

Choosing love, choosing to believe that I am not just long legs and big tits with a mighty active and highly conditioned brain - it hurt. It stretched and pulled me in ways I never knew possible. Some days I felt such pain I literally thought I would die. Letting go of my negative programming and what I thought to be my truth and stepping into the new truth that I am fundamentally pure was like removing all my skin and going through the discomfort and pain and itch of waiting for the new skin to grow. I have never had a face peel but I would imagine it's pretty terrifying and uncomfortable. So that will be my metaphor for moving from old me to new me. It hurt.

And it was the most natural, simple, easy thing to do - because it is my truth.

Don't get me wrong though - as supportive as my S-Team is, they test and challenge me regularly. Daily!

When I was unconscious, it could be argued that life was easier. (Except that I was anxious, a victim, in unhealthy relationships and totally off course in terms of my purpose!) These days, I am up for the challenge and my S-Team knows it! They shine a light on my 'stuff' at any opportunity. I see meaning in everything because I know my Guides are always showing me new ways to view and experience life. I am conscious to the importance of choosing my thoughts carefully because the universe hears me and delivers!

Choosing to jump on board with my Spirit Team was no small decision. It was a leap into the unknown and it felt scary at first. I would sit in guided meditation with my Spiritual Coaches and feel scared because entering this new world was so unknown to me. And yet it felt the most natural course to take. Clearly the way I was unconsciously bumbling through life thinking I was alone didn't serve me. So I was willing to give this spiritual stuff a shot. And I found my home.

And to be clear, my spiritual home is unique and personal to me. What I feel comfortable in may be different to you. There's a lot on offer in terms of Spirituality - from Buddhism to Shamanism, Christianity to Kabbalah, Numerology to Astrology, Meditation to Yoga - and from my point of view it's about finding meaning and committing to a life of personal transformation as I move closer and closer to the original truth of me - that I am love.

This isn't a book about spirituality and what is on offer. I am far from an expert on the subject and there are people far more qualified and expert than me to write about it.

This isn't a book to tell you what you should or shouldn't be doing in terms of exploring your own spirituality either. I do encourage you to search out your meaning from all that is on offer. I also encourage you to stick to what feels true and right for you. Go with what feels right, in your gut and in your heart. Listen to your Spirit - she will guide you. After all, all that is real is your Spirit.

If your intention is personal growth and a journey to get closer to the truth that you are love, your Spirit will show you the way - and if that means you are attracted to a statue of an elephant and know that the Buddhist tradition believes that figure will bring you good luck, then go for it. May that elephant inspire you to bravely move more deeply towards your truth.

My only offering is to suggest you do not look outside of yourself for all your answers. Your answers are within you - you are a mighty powerful being, full of truth. Use what you are drawn to and what lights you up as tools to unlock your own truths. No one else can tell you how to live your life. It is your life! Your job is to find tools and techniques that allow you to access your own truth.

You may sometimes like the guidance of an alternative therapist to help you uncover your truth when you are feeling stuck. And I say, what's the harm in that? If getting your tarot cards read turns you on or you enjoy a bit of Reiki or perhaps you want to tune into a passed-over relative for your answers, go for it. Again, check in with your gut in terms of how you are using these intuitive people. Is it a crutch? Are you avoiding your own process and looking for a quick fix? Or do you have access to a really authentic healer who is able to support you in moving through your block with more ease and grace? I find that a healer or alternative therapist will usually tell me what I already know to be true - they tend to clinch it for me.

When it comes to selecting any kind of healer or psychic or new-age therapist, just go with your gut. If they feel honest and authentic and caring, go for it. If it feels off in any way, trust that.

So by all means, explore different spiritual paths. Allow all of your spiritual experiences to be uniquely yours. Allow the way you connect with and process your spirituality to be personal to you. And never forget your truth is within you.

Always follow your gut!

In my experience, if someone tells me their way is the only way....I walk in the opposite direction. And if they tell me I am a sinner, I grab a bottle of wine and run a mile!

So, going back to my S-Team. I would like to tell you a little more about how I perceive them.

GOD / THE UNIVERSE / THE LIGHT

I couldn't explain God any better than Mike Dooley does in this passage from his book, "Leveraging the Universe":

"I realize I'm not using the term "God" here in any conventional sense, but rather as defined by the Truth of Being that everything is God. And by this

definition, God includes your chosen focus and thoughts. I think what most people want, however, is to believe in a God that has a personality – and not just any personality but one that is similar to their own. But while thinking that God has a personality offers a simplistic and manageable view of the Creator, it also implies that the Creator might also be judgemental, which negates the simple and otherwise obvious Truths of Being already laid out – in particular, the truth that There is only Love.

Of course I believe in "God", and of course I believe "It" must have some kind of faculty for unconditional love, far exceeding in beauty and support the type of love expressed by humans, but I'm very comfortable with the parallel realization that there is no such God as the one most of us were raised to believe in. And while I certainly can't wrap my head around the entirety of what God is, I can, like you, at least observe what is and what feels right and act accordingly, without having to think of God as a man or woman, happy or angry, demanding or judgemental."

I use the terms God, the Universe and the Light interchangeably. And others will have other names, no doubt! The Universe is everything. It is a non-physical power that is love and that permeates all things. It is all matter and it is the space between all matter. So it is me and it surrounds me and it connects me to everything and everyone. It is intelligent and it is creative. It creates from the directive of our thoughts. Yes, we are that powerful! (More on that later in the book.)

To connect with the Light is like going home. As I mentioned earlier, there are a myriad of spiritual practices on offer to take you there. Meditations and guided visualisations work for me – they allow me to sit in the presence of my source and all that I know I am. To be in that space gives my physical mind and body a rest and helps to remind me that I am so much more than just human. It's an opportunity to sit in the presence of pure love and feel myself as pure love. It is delicious! I encourage you to discover your own way of connecting with the Light.

My intention every day is to live in the Light. I know that is where my healing can be found and anything that is not of highest service to me can be released to the Light for transformation. The Light is where I am supported to grow and encouraged to create. In the Light I am able to be my authentic self and to feel completely unleashed, easy and free.

When I say "Thank you, Universe," I am acknowledging the intelligent, creative, loving force that has brought me my desire and I am acknowledging the role I played in bringing that desire into my awareness. I thank God a lot these days!

SPIRIT GUIDES

I love these guys! I've only met one of my Guides properly but have been told by several intuitive people that I have several Guides. I know it in my gut - I just haven't taken the time, if I am honest, to get to know them all. My masseuse even tunes into them for guidance on where my body needs healing. They guide her to just the right spots and help her to see how my chakras need balancing and where my energy is out of whack. They know me better than I know myself so I just hand it over to them when I jump onto the massage table and I feel wonderful afterwards!

The Guide I have met is a warrior princess. Yep! It surprised me too. Joanna is awesome. So strong and yet so feminine. She yields a sword that protects me and serves to remind me of just how powerful I am. Her long white Grecian robes give me permission to step into my feminine, surrendered essence. I sense her laughing as I type this. She knows I know her and she knows that I still find it all a little 'out there'. And yet I often call on her and she guides me. I've known her a few years and yet I am still getting to know her. I am still opening up to her presence. The other day I questioned if she was real and asked for a sign. In that very moment I turned my head to see Starbucks logos everywhere. I know the Starbucks lady is a mermaid called Siren, but in that moment she was Joanna. She had the look of a warrior princess. I only had to go home and Google 'Starbucks logo' to discover this about Siren, the twin-tailed mermaid:

"In a lot of ways, she's a muse - always there, inspiring us and pushing us

ahead. And she's a promise too, inviting all of us to find what we're looking for, even if it's something we haven't even imagined yet."

And THAT is what I love about our Guides. They wink at us! They are deep and they want us to know our truth. They also have a lightness of being and a sense of humour - well, at least in my experience they do!

So let's break it down. I would love for you to get to know your Spirit Guides too.

WHAT IS A SPIRIT GUIDE?

A non-physical being selected by your Spirit or Higher Self to guide you through your human experience.

Their role is to support and guide you to fulfill the purpose you chose before being born.

They take on many appearances. Some people have rather exotic Guides - Native American Indians or Tibetan Monks; others have more regular Guides - an old man or a nurse.

Guides are energetic beings so they don't exactly have a sex but they do tend to take on a male or female energy, which you will be able to sense.

You can have more than one Guide. Some stay with you your entire life. Some pop in and out of your life as and when you need them.

Some Guides are more evolved than others. You may have a highly ascended master such as Jesus or Buddha on your team. Or you may have more simple spirits who have a mastery in some area that you knew you would need in this lifetime. You may even have a deceased relative on your team.

They communicate with you in a way that will be unique to you and it will take practice to discover how you can interpret their messages. After some practice, eventually you will be able to just close your eyes and call on your Guide for advice whenever you need it.

HOW DO WE RECEIVE MESSAGES FROM OUR GUIDES?

- Intuition – how you receive a gut feeling will depend largely on whether you are clairvoyant (see images), claircognizant ('just know'), clairaudient (hear a message) or clairsentient (feel it in your body).

- Signs – signals, synchronicities and signs will often come to you repeatedly until you interpret them. The key is to pay attention! If you are not sure a sign is 'real', just ask that it be shown to you again in some way so that you 'know' it is the truth, in no uncertain terms!

- Dreams – often a feeling from a dream will help to guide our next steps or give us an answer.

- Send someone to you – Coincidentally someone will come into your life that will give you a clue or answer you needed.

- Nudging – circumstances out of your control may happen which ensure you are in a certain place at a certain time.

TOOLS TO CONNECT WITH YOUR GUIDES

- Journalling (great if you are clairaudient) – write (typed or handwritten) until you 'know' the dialogue is coming from your Guide.

- Meditation – tune into the frequency of your Guide and ask for a message or an answer to a question. Keep asking questions and hearing answers until you 'know' the answer is coming from your guide. The answers will be given to you in a way that will match your intuitive modality.

- Dreams – ask that an answer be given to you while you sleep. How you 'felt' about a dream will guide you to the answer you were looking for.

- Divination tools – some people like to use pendulums, tarot cards or muscle testing, among other things.

Learn to listen to your intuition!

Take notice of signs and synchronicities!

Ask a trusted psychic to help you.

Remember, often a Guide will not give you an exact answer. Rather, you may be given an opportunity to work something out for yourself by receiving signs and signals to direct you towards the answer. You didn't choose a life on earth that was easy! You were looking for a challenge, to help you to grow. So all the answers and situations you want will not be neatly placed in your lap. You will be given hunches and clues to guide you towards the next step, enabling you to work things out for yourself, which will assure you of the deepest level of understanding, learning and evolution. That is what your Spirit wants!

 *A MEDITATION*

The Spirit Guide Meditation – you can download the audio of this meditation for free at: http://daringandmighty.com/meditation-library

Prepare your meditation space, light a candle and enjoy this beautiful 20-minute visualisation whenever you desire to connect with your Spirit Guides.

When you have completed the meditation, grab your journal and make some notes about the special experience you just had.

ANGELS

I honestly don't feel qualified to write about Angels. I know I have them supporting me and I sometimes feel them working with me and around me. Sometimes in meditation, I just 'know' they are with me and can often feel a tingling on a part of my body and know they are working on me in some way. Something like psychic surgery. Healing what needs to be healed.

If I ever need to know anything about Angels, I refer to books by the likes of Kyle Gray and Doreen Virtue. I also have a friend, Anna Taylor, who calls herself 'The Angels' Voice'. These people live and breathe Angels. They have been blessed with a relationship to these beings of light that is incredibly humbling.

When it comes to Angels, I keep it pretty simple. Most of my knowledge comes from a children's book I bought for my son! It's called 'Thank you, Angels', by Doreen Virtue. My son seems to think that Angels are totally natural. I on the other hand have had to battle against it all feeling a little weird because the ease of believing in a higher power tends to be weeded out of us at a young age. It's not easily understood, so best to just ignore it and accept we are alone, right?! And how has that worked out for us...?!

As my awareness of myself as a Spirit has grown, so too has my awareness of the presence of Angels. I can't really explain it. I just *know*. And that knowing is my intuition - that sixth sense, which I have come to trust implicitly.

I call on my Angels to protect me regularly. When I get in an aeroplane, I thank the Angels for protecting the aircraft. When I am headed out on a date, I thank the Angels for ensuring the best of both of us is revealed. When I am about to meet someone that I know I allow to have me feel small or weak, I thank the Angels for surrounding me with their white light of protection, keeping safe my sense of self.

Last winter I had to collect my son from school and we had a sudden, unexpected, very heavy dump of snow. My car is NOT built for the snow. But I had to get to school. I was petrified of the drive and I was praying to the Angels over and over during the journey. I reached a section of the drive where there is an intersection and the traffic is always very heavy. My car lost control and began to spin. My brakes didn't work. I had no control except to pray. My car skidded in a full circle three times on the wrong side of the road. It all happened in dead-slow motion. I kept praying as I expected to be hit by oncoming traffic on this notoriously busy road. Miraculously all traffic disappeared and the car spun itself to a nice safe parking spot at the side of the road. At the precise moment my car stopped, a dear friend called my mobile and her first words were, 'Are you ok?' She called to see if I needed help getting my son from school. I burst into tears. I knew the Angels were with me.

The other day my car ran out of petrol while driving to visit a friend in hospital who really needed cheering up. We were already running late! My son and I were forced to pull over to the side of the road, just 100 metres from the petrol station. I asked the Angels for one final push because we simply could not miss hospital visiting hours! The car started and we got to within 10 metres of the garage before stopping, embarrassingly, in the middle of a very busy road and immediately a man appeared and pushed us the last few metres. We re-fueled, grabbed some chocolatey goodies for my friend and headed to the hospital. Thank you, Angels!

Another time I simply could not start the lawnmower. I tried and tried and tried. I was exhausted by pulling that cord over and over again. I had probably by this point flooded the engine too and I swear I was about to give myself a hernia! I said to my son, 'Let's call on the Angels.' In total and utter faith, he closed his eyes and said, 'Please Angels, start the motor,' and on the first pull, with very little energy left in me, it started!

I could go on and on with stories about how I have been saved by Angels. I even have a story about how I called on Archangel Michael to remove a Spirit from my home. What I witnessed was a miracle but that's something I can't explain in words.

I am no expert, but I know my Angels are with me. I know we are not alone. I know they desire to support us to live a life on purpose and in love.

In fact, immediately before starting to write this section on Angels, I went to my trusty pack of Doreen Virtue Archangel Oracle Cards. I use these cards religiously and they unfailingly tell me what I need to hear. Indeed, the answers are invariably what I already sensed to be the truth. I just needed another 'sign'! (Oh ye of little faith!)

I pulled a card before writing because I didn't feel 'qualified' to write about Angels and wanted some guidance on whether it was appropriate for me to proceed with this piece. Here's what I got:

COUNSELLOR

Archangel Azrael:

"You are a natural counsellor, and many people benefit from your guidance and reassurance. Your life purpose involves counseling people in ways that uplift, motivate, comfort, heal, and inspire. You're a true spiritual counsellor, and people find you to be a trustworthy confidante. Expand your counselling work to the next level, because you're about to help greater numbers of people. Call upon me for guidance and support."

Well blow me down!

It turns out that Archangel Azrael's name means, "Whom God Helps", and he helps those who are helpers.

So how can you communicate with your Angels? Well, I am not sure there is a right or wrong way. It's a personal relationship so my instinct would be to say do it in a way that feels right for you. Remember, you are a feeler now, not a thinker!

I love how Kyle Gray suggests we talk to our Angels. He doesn't ask them for stuff. He has total faith and trust that what is right for him will be delivered by his Angels. So instead of asking, he thanks them. That feels really good to me too.

So, instead of asking for a sign that they are with you, you can say:

"Thank you, Angels for reminding me of your presence."

Or, instead of asking for help, you can say:

"Thank you, Angels for supporting me."

Or, whenever you are feeling doubt, you can say:

"Thank you, Angels for revealing to me what I need to know."

Then trust your gut. Trust the first thing you feel to be your answer. Or allow some time and trust the answer will be shown to you with total clarity over the coming minutes, hours or days. You will 'know' what is meant for you.

My Angel Cards are uncanny and they unfailingly give me the answers I desire. It may not always be what I hope to read. It is, however, what I always know to be true for me in the moment! Thank you, Angels!

I am... YOUR AFFIRMATIONS

I trust myself.

I trust my Spirit Team.

I am held safe by a loving Universe.

My Guides and Angels have my back.

 *PUMP UP THE VOLUME*

"Angel" - Sarah McLachlan

"I Know" - Jude

"If God Will Send His Angels" - U2

"God" - Gary Barlow

Self-Love

I close my eyes

to connect to source

to my True Self.

I travel home.

Weightless.

Tingling.

Expanded.

I am pure love.

Pure Spirit.

Just perfect.

Katie Phillips

Daring and Mighty lady! I dare you to love yourself and live a Mighty life!

I have a feeling you are up for this challenge! But first....

You have come a long way already and have been working so hard at understanding who you are. This process is not for the faint of heart and I want to remind you at this point just how special you are for undertaking this journey. In fact, I would like to encourage you to take time out to congratulate yourself for how far you have come. If you have been doing the work assigned in this book, then you deserve to be congratulated. So, before you read any further, I wonder what you could do to honour the work you have done so far?

How could you treat yourself? What do you desire? What would light you up? What would make you feel cherished?

Perhaps a long soak in a lovely candle-lit bath? As you lie there, congratulate yourself for your achievements so far.

Perhaps a celebration dinner? You could dine alone or with a partner or even host a party in your honour! You have much to celebrate!

Maybe you desire a new pair of shoes or a new outfit. Make the purchase with intention. This is a special gift to yourself for being brave enough to take control of your life.

You may like to create a very simple ritual such as lighting a candle and stating out loud all that you have achieved and why you are so proud of yourself. Perhaps write this down in your journal and declare your gratitude for you!

Whatever you choose to do, remember to be intentional about the celebration and the gift you are giving yourself. I cannot stress enough how important it is to celebrate every step of your Self-Love Affair. We tend to focus on what we haven't achieved rather than focus on what we have. As you will discover in upcoming chapters, you get what you focus on! So why not choose today to focus your energy into recognising how far you have come? Give yourself a gold star! And know that as you do this, you are energetically attracting more to be thankful for.

Self-recognition is a big part of what it means to love yourself. Praising yourself lifts up your Spirit. I bet you have had a pattern of criticising yourself for a very long time now. I know you are done with that! I know you must be so fed up with that self-abuse, which, quite simply, breaks your Spirit. So whether you feel deserving of celebrating yourself or not, I encourage you to do it.

Choose to create a new habit. If you feel blocked by a persistent belief around not being worthy of recognition or feeling guilty for treating yourself, I encourage you to do the work to dig deeper into where those limiting beliefs have come from and then choose to transform them. Go back to Part One of this book and do the exercises in the chapters 'Who Is the Captain Of Your Life?' and 'Hello Super Woman!' Get into reality about why you feel unworthy and then forgive yourself for allowing yourself to feel this way for so long. You know it's time to let that belief go and move forward. It's time to create a new story. It's time to do life differently. It's time to love yourself!

"God extended himself in love, and we are all expressions of this love. This is the Original Blessing we share with each other. There are no exceptions to this. None. The basic truth about you is 'I am loveable'. Everybody's basic truth is 'I am loveable'. This is true whether you remember or forget it. It is also true whether you believe it or not." Robert Holden ('Loveability')

Before I write any more around what self-love is and how you can love yourself more, I want to ask you a question.

Do you feel guilty around the concept of loving yourself?

For some reason the words 'self-love' have been attached to concepts of egocentricity, shamefulness and selfishness and I want to bust that belief straight up.

Not only does self-love benefit you, it benefits anyone that comes into contact with you. It also has a ripple effect that will benefit person after person after person that you will probably never meet or even know to exist. Your love for yourself will stretch far and wide. You will never know the extent to which the wonderful power of loving yourself has on the world. It is just awesome! Such is the nature of love. And the awesome truth is that you ARE love.

You are pure, perfect Spirit. You are therefore pure, perfect love.

What's not to love about that?

And if you are love, then surely it makes sense that your purpose on this planet is to love? Where better to start than with you?

Your mission is to BE love. The work you have done to date to clear away anything that doesn't feel true to you has been the work to remove any fear cloaking the perfection of your love.

Now that you have begun removing your layers of conditioning and programming (and you will continue to do this more and more now that you are an awakened, conscious woman), you are able to step out into the world as the love bomb that you truly are!

Your assignment from this day forward is to stop self-abandoning. Your mission is to remember the truth of who you are – in every moment, in every decision, in every spoken word. Remember that you are a beautiful, perfect, non-judgemental spiritual being.

You are love.

Loving yourself is about unconditionally accepting and understanding all the parts of you – positive and negative. It's about loving your light and your dark. It means becoming your own best friend!

Lady, you can be so mean to yourself! If you think some of the 'unhelpful stuff' you have inherited from previous generations was tough, well that simply pails into insignificance when you consider how horrible you can be to yourself. You would never treat your best mate the way you treat yourself. You would never say those nasty things that you tell yourself. It's time to give yourself the benefit of the doubt. It's time to give yourself a break!

Be honest. How often do you show yourself compassion? How respectful are you of you? How gently do you treat yourself? How forgiving are you when you make a mistake? It's cringeworthy, isn't it, just how nasty we can be to ourselves?!

Choosing to love yourself means the following become compulsory:

Self-Care

Self-Understanding

Self-Compassion

Self-Connection

Choosing to love yourself means intentionally honouring all parts of you every single day:

Your wondrous body

Your beautiful mind

Your delightful inner child

Your spectacular Spirit

Choosing to love yourself means caring for your body, understanding your thoughts, having compassion for your feelings and developing a relationship with your Spirit.

Self-love requires you to become an expert at receiving. As a woman you are by your very nature designed to receive and yet most women spend a lot of time in the masculine energy of 'do do do', 'think think think', 'achieve achieve achieve'! In our effort to be 'equals', we have forgotten how to be women! Mastering the divine art of receiving is an integral part of learning to love yourself. Asking for help is a biggie for many women, meaning that receiving support is a skill to be developed!

No matter what it is you desire, you will need to make yourself available to receive it - which takes practice if you are conditioned to always be in action overdrive. So whether you desire health, abundance, love, adventure, beauty, friendship, happiness, freedom, understanding, travel....whatever it is for you, the key is to be available to receive it. If there is a block to your ability to receive something, your work is to go back to basics and understand what it is and where it came from, then choose to release yourself into a more loving belief that will serve you.

Your willingness to being open to receive is crucial to loving yourself.

A desire to honour all parts of you allows you to be available for yourself.

It means being available to receive YOU.

Do you dare?

Yes?!

Fabulous. So let's break it down.

1. CARING FOR YOUR WONDROUS BODY

Your body is the guardian of your soul. It's your HQ! It is the vehicle that allows you to have this awesome human experience. It is literally the house in which you live. So it goes without saying how important it is to honour and respect your physical self!

Your body is a marvellous instrument!

It allows you to experience your feelings in a physical way - from tantalising ecstasy to heart pumping adventure to belly busting laughter to salty tears and hot rage.

It allows you to experience your environment - this beautiful world, which is your playground for spiritual expansion! From enjoying delicious flavours to witnessing spectacular sunsets to the warmth of a hug and the glorious sound of children playing.

Your body is also your barometer. In the same way that the meteorological instrument measures atmospheric pressure, your body very intelligently mirrors the pressure of your inner world. When you are emotionally clean and clear and spiritually happy and healthy, you glow! You feel light and almost literally *shine* a light (which ties into that self-love ripple effect I was speaking of earlier!). When you are emotionally blocked and spiritually broken, you look dull and feel heavy. This could show up as disease, premature aging, weight gain, aches and pains, acne, tiredness, inability to concentrate, headaches ... I could go on and on. You get the idea.

You are meant to be healthy! If you are not, it is a sign that something is out of whack and it is usually a sign that your emotional, mental or spiritual health is off balance. I know that if I have a sore throat, I am probably not speaking my truth in an area of my life. If I have back ache or sore shoulders, I am carrying a burden of some description that needs to be released; it is often a sign that more support is required in my life. If I get a pimple I can often link that to some level of anger - either towards myself or others. A stye in my eye is often a sign that I haven't processed a sadness and could probably do with a good cry!

I love the work of Louise Hay and Dr. Candace Pert around this topic and there are many others who have studied the impact that thoughts and feelings have on our physical health. If this interests you, then I encourage you to do your own research. Self-love is about taking an interest in yourself! We live in such an exciting era with so much information available at our fingertips. Do yourself a favour and learn about your beautiful body - get conscious around how it works and how you can live with more kindness to yourself.

At the very least, make the decision to be kind to your body. It's pretty simple and obvious stuff:

- Take naps and enjoy some early nights.

- If you currently do not exercise at all, do yourself a favour and respect your body enough to keep it strong and supple by at least taking regular walks. If that means getting off the bus one stop early or parking your car a few hundred metres further from your destination, do that.

- Eat healthily. You know the drill! At the very minimum, reduce alcohol, caffeine and sugar. Increase your greens and water. Cut the stimulants. Increase the nutrients. Simples!

- Express your emotions. Repressed emotions cause blockages in your body. Anger is not bad! It is natural. So give it room to be and let it out. Scream into a pillow, punch a punching bag, watch a sad film and have a good cry or write a really angry letter, then burn it.

Love yourself enough to notice what you are putting into your body – and notice your reason why. Are you over-eating to push down an emotion? Are you taking drugs to block out a fear? Are you lying on the couch watching box sets to avoid social interaction? What are you using to numb your pain? What do you not want to face? What are you avoiding feeling?

The likelihood that an addictive or numbing behaviour is the reason behind you not exercising or eating properly or expressing your emotions or getting enough sleep is pretty high. You are now a conscious woman who has chosen to take responsibility for her life. I trust you to address any numbing habits with kindness, compassion and understanding.

Taking simple steps around sleep, diet, exercise and expression will mean you are living within a body that is the best version of you. The more you consciously take care of your body, the better you will feel about yourself. As you learn to listen to your body and develop a kind and loving relationship with it, the more forgiving and less critical you will be. We forgive and accept what we love. We criticise and judge what we dislike. I urge you to love the body you were given. Your body – its shape and size and colour – is your gift. It is another opportunity for your Spirit to expand and evolve. If a lesson for you in this lifetime is to learn self-acceptance and self-love, you may well have been gifted a particular body to help you to learn that deep lesson. Unconditional love is the goal.

Self-care is the aim of the game when it comes to your physical well-being. How you care for your body will be unique to you and I encourage you to consciously choose ways to nurture and pamper yourself. Indeed, I encourage you to practise the feminine art of receiving! Here are some ideas – and do go ahead and discover your own:

- have regular massages

- walk in the woods

- go to the gym

- run on the beach

- have a facial

- book a reflexology session

- enjoy some Reiki healing

- book an aromatherapy session

- have your groceries delivered or have someone carry them to your car

- ask your partner to cook you a healthy meal

- enjoy a long hot bath

- go for a swim

- sit in the steam room

- do a detoxifying cleanse

- book an appointment with a nutritionist

- have your nails done

- book in regular hairdressing appointments

- clean your make-up brushes

- book an OB/GYN appointment

- get waxed!

- visit the dentist

- buy new knickers!

Self-care is not rocket science. I know you know that!

Give yourself permission to take care of your wondrous body.

Love yourself enough to honour the vehicle that can transport you to your deepest desires.

2. UNDERSTANDING YOUR BEAUTIFUL MIND

You have the most wonderful mind and it serves you in so many miraculous ways. Yet we do seem to give our minds such a bad rap, don't we. They seem to be the source of frustration, judgement, criticism, stress, doubt and confusion. Our heads get so full up with noise and to-do lists we don't know whether we are coming or going. So we say things like, 'My head hurts!' or 'I'm brain dead' or 'I am so over my thoughts'. We get cross with ourselves for having such a mean mind and frustrated with ourselves for not being able to contain all the information we think we ought to be able to manage. We beat ourselves up and blame our 'stupid head'.

Do you feel how low the energy just got as you read that? Heavy, huh!

We are SO hard on ourselves!

We forget that our awesome mind can be the source of our joy, delight and peace. We forget that our incredible mind has the power to guide our life anywhere we desire it to go.

If we beat up on it, we don't stand a chance.

If we nurture and understand it, the world is suddenly our oyster!

When we love our mind we achieve mental health!

Right now I invite you to make the decision to be kind to your mind. It is as real and valid a part of you as your heart, your soul and your body.

Choose to honour your mind. Choose to accept it with compassion and understanding. After all, you have discovered that many of the thoughts you have are inherited and don't even belong to you. You also learned how to let those go. From this moment onwards, you get to choose your own thoughts and they can be kind, loving and of service to you. The choice is yours!

Choose today to stop being so hard on yourself!

Choose to stop comparing yourself to others. Decide today to mind your own business!

Choose positive words and be kind to yourself with your choice of language.

Commit to only having positive inner talk. Choose to build your inner strength with words of affirmation. Speak to yourself as you would to a child – with compassion and love.

Quit filling your head with lists. If you have things to do, write them down and free up your mind. Give it room to breathe, to desire, to dream!

Forgive your mind for thoughts and beliefs that have damaged and hurt you or others. Whatever you think you have or haven't done – forgive yourself. Release them into love and be available for healing. Allow yourself to be in the present because in this very moment, you are a clean slate. Forgiveness allows you to create from that clean and clear space.

If you have held fear-based beliefs like "I am not good enough' or 'I am not loveable' or 'I can't trust others' or 'I am damaged' you can choose today to forgive yourself for believing such things. You can simply make the decision to choose love-based beliefs that will guide your life in the direction you truly desire. You are not a victim to your programming.

You can choose to re-parent your mind!

Remember, forgiveness is simply a choice. Showing a willingness to create loving thoughts and beliefs means the wheels are already in motion. That new 'muscle' is being built. With self-compassion and kindness you can allow your new thoughts to build strength and momentum. In time, you will be an unstoppable, positive force!

Choose to be positive. I don't mean to put on a brave face or pretend to be ok! Accepting, allowing and feeling your feelings is crucial. And sometimes you have tough days and they need to be acknowledged. As I have said many times, the key to self-love is to be kind to yourself. Choosing to be positive is simply another way to be intentionally kind to yourself. It may seem childishly simple but literally setting a morning intention like 'I choose to be positive today' will dramatically affect the way you approach every single aspect of your day. It will help you to shift a thought like 'The car park will be jammed; I will never get a spot' to 'I bet I bag a rock-star park today!' It will support you in making choices around who you spend your time with and help guide you to people who are loving and respectful. It will have you view experiences in a positive light and difficulties as a gift of love and an opportunity for growth rather than have you drop back into the low vibrational belief that 'life is hard'. It will assist you when making choices around what food to put into your body and whether to go to the pub or a yoga class. When you intend positivity, it affects every single aspect of your life. It's cool! What's not to love?!

I would like to encourage you to be mindful of what you allow your mind to absorb. Your beautiful mind requires stimulation just as much as relaxation so it's important to get conscious about what you let into your head and in what quantities. Studying and learning is a great way to stimulate your mind. You can even exercise it with puzzles like crosswords or sudoku.

Discover what works for you in terms of relaxing your mind. Meditation, conscious breathing, walking and gentle exercise allows the mind to be calm. Just choosing to close your eyes or look out of the window can also relax your mind. Or you could experiment with alternative healing arts such as aromatherapy and colour therapy for mind relaxation (and stimulation).

Taking responsibility for what you allow into your mind is key. You know how sometimes when you are watching a movie or TV show you get so engrossed in it that you lose yourself and almost become part of the drama unfolding on the screen? Well, did you know that your mind doesn't know the difference between watching a TV show and accepting the content of that show as your reality? This is especially applicable to small children. Freaky, huh!

Choose to fill your beautiful mind with things that are kind, supportive and nurturing. Stop self-abandoning and scaring yourself! Be there for you.

Loving your mind means choosing your desires over your 'shoulds'! There is a chapter coming up soon around assessing your values which will really help to alleviate any 'shoulding' that you do. For now, I encourage you to notice when you say you 'should' do something and consider what you 'desire' to do instead. Choose to stop being so demanding and hard on yourself. Listen to the chat in your head that instructs and orders you about. Choose to be kinder to yourself and trust your desires...because they are the voice of your soul!

We are so conditioned to listen to our head, as if what goes on in there is gospel - the truth, the only truth, so help you God! The real truth is that our Spirit has our answers and is our best guidance system. So I encourage you to tune out of your head and into your heart as often as possible. If you go into head overwhelm, put a hand on your heart centre. You can do this by running your fingers down your breastbone, in between your breasts, and you will know when you hit 'the spot' - it will just feel right. You will feel connected in some way. When you are there, take a few deep breaths and then ask your heart what the next right move is for you or what you desire to do. The first thing you hear is your answer.

Your intellect is awesome and necessary. However, as a conscious woman who has decided to love herself, you can choose to turn down the volume on the critical, judgemental chatter and turn up the volume of your heart and your soul.

It's a pretty cool choice to have, don't you think?!

Shoulding is exhausting. Listening to your heart is such a relief!

Do what you love. Only you are blocking you from having all that you desire.

Looking after your precious mind is pretty simple really. I am sure I haven't told you much that you didn't already know. Again, it comes back to permission. Can you give yourself permission to take loving care of your mind?

Your power is within your thoughts. Love yourself enough to honour the force behind the creation of all that you desire.

3. SHOWING COMPASSION FOR YOUR DELIGHTFUL INNER CHILD

As you have already discovered, you are the vulnerable little girl within you. Your emotional self now is very connected to who you were and how you felt as a child. Your child inside is very real and she needs your attention, just as much as all the other aspects of your self.

Self-love requires us to listen to the voice of our inner child. To hear her when she is feeling alone, unloveable, worried, insecure, too much or unsafe. If she knows she is being heard and if we can offer her love and understanding and a space to express her tough feelings, she will feel empowered to also express her joy and playfulness.

From this moment on I invite you to treat yourself as you would a small child - with compassion, understanding and unconditional love.

I find it so much easier to accept my feelings when I consider that they are coming from the child inside me. I am instantly able to quit being hard on myself and switch to patience and compassion. I will often take time out simply to listen in to the voice of my child. I will consciously connect with her and ask her how she is and if she needs anything from me. Essentially what I am doing is asking myself how I am feeling. I give myself a chance to be honest and admit if I am feeling a little low or flat or cross and I make a decision around how to manage that feeling. What do I need? Do I need a hug? Do I need to talk to a friend? Do I need a nap or a day off work? Do I need to do some journalling or bash the stuffing out of a pillow?! You get the idea. As a conscious woman who can trust herself, I know what I need to do to allow my feelings and give them room to be. And so do you.

Sometimes my inner child is full of joy and sparkle and is asking me to go and have some fun! Again, this is another permission piece. Can I love myself enough to take time for joy and play? It's a perfect opportunity to get the Lego out with my son or take a trip away or arrange a girls' night out!

As you now know, our society isn't too comfortable with the expression of emotions. We bury our feelings and are encouraged not to cry. We are told not to be angry - to take a deep breath, relax and be calm!

It's not working! It's why we suffer so much dis-ease. As a society we are repressed and depressed. We are sick and tired. And we yearn for happiness.

Lucky lady, you know the secret! Happiness is found within self-acceptance. That means allowing yourself to feel the way you feel. Give yourself permission!

(Are you cottoning on to the themes here around permission and choice?!)

If you feel angry, it's ok! BE angry! Don't go and do a yoga class and suppress your anger. Choose to let it out. Bash, run, swear, dance, write it out. The way you let it free is up to you and you know how important it is to do that in a way that is safe and respectful. No more screaming at poor innocent waiters!

If you feel sad and know you could do with a good cry, rent yourself a chick flick and bawl your eyes out. Sob and wail. It's allowed!

Whatever you feel, remember it will pass. Feelings never last. You are an energetic being, meaning you are always in a state of flow. You are ever changing. You can trust that your feelings will change. Your assignment is simply to pass through the emotion. Feel it until you don't feel it anymore. Quit trying to dodge it through sophisticated avoidance strategies like work or food or television or drugs. Suck it up and sit in the feeling. I promise you, you will feel better afterwards!

And remember, what we resist persists. Avoiding a feeling only means it will bite you harder on the bum another time. Learning to tune into your feelings regularly means they are easier to feel and move through. In the early days of doing this work it could take a little time to work through some stuff - that's because the feelings have been building and compounding for years and years. After a while, it gets easier. There is less to work through. It kinda becomes like routine maintenance rather than a major emotional overhaul!

I invite you to commit to honouring your feelings. Allow them. Give them time and space to be heard and expressed. Create safe, loving space for that to happen.

Love yourself enough to develop a compassionate relationship with your inner child. She is desperate for your attention!

4. CONNECTING TO YOUR SPECTACULAR SPIRIT

We focussed earlier on your body and the idea that your body is your headquarters. It's not who you are! As you now know, you are your Spirit.

Your Spirit is your unconditioned self. It is the truth of who you are. It is pure, peaceful and innocent. It is unshakeable, perfect and eternal. It is love.

When you have a relationship with your Spirit, you are able to relax and just be you because you have stopped judging yourself. The criticism stops. That loud noise in your head calms down. You are free to just be. You feel safe and at home. It's a wonderful feeling!

We learn to be in relationship with our conditioned self – our ego or personality – rather than our Spirit. We identify with our body rather than our Spirit. We believe we are separate from all and alone. We forget that we are part of a whole – that we are all one and connected.

Identifying with our ego-self rather than our Spirit causes major anxiety because we are identifying with something that doesn't really exist so we feel lost and unsafe. We search for something that will have us feel found and secure. We look for anything that will fulfill us and complete us and have us feel as if we exist – whether that's another person or a job or food. We search and search and search but nothing can satiate the desire to be unconditionally validated and loved because when we identify with ego, we are conditioned to never stop searching for that feeling of perfect fulfillment...because in ego it doesn't exist.

That feeling is only found when we learn to identify with our True Self – to lean into our Spirit.

When I discovered my Spirit and my Truth, I was able to breathe a huge sigh of relief. And that is what I desire for you too!

Our ego is very competitive and highly judgemental. It's exhausting. Our ego tells us that we are wrong or not enough (compared to what?!) and because we are physical beings, it's our body that gets attacked the most! 'You are fat! You have clearly eaten too many pies!' 'Jeez, you are skinny! You had better sort that out.' 'You really need to get to the hairdresser!' 'Oof, you better not let him see you naked because *that* is not a pretty sight!' 'Really!? You are going to wear *that*?' And it goes on and on and on.

When we hear a judgement from our ego, because we perceive it to be who we are, we listen up as if it's the truth. But it's not our truth. Our truth wouldn't judge us to be anything – good or bad. We just are. And we are more than enough!

Our ego tricks us too. Some days, the ego can seem rather nice. We have a good hair day and our skin is glowing. We get a nice big tick. We feel great as a result. Then we have a day of bird's nest hair and spots and the ego tells us we are 'bad' in some way. But we are neither good nor bad. Both are judgements. The yo-yo between the two, good and bad, is exhausting.

Your Spirit is constant. There is no yo-yo. In Spirit you are always perfect just as you are. You are seen. You are not judged. It's such a relief!

When in relationship to ego we are always striving to be better. To be more perfect. To always have a 'good' day! We work hard toward this ideal of perfection because when we get there, we think we will be happy. But there is no such thing as perfection. When you are relating to ego, even the perceived perfection is a judgement, meaning you can never be perfect enough. It is seriously tiring.

Striving for perfection means you are often keeping up appearances. How many people do you know who smile a lot and tell you they are ok but underneath are suffering deeply? Not only are we judging ourselves but we are expecting judgement from others. After all, they are egos too. So we strive to be perfect in front of them. And just when you thought judging yourself and being judged by others was hard enough, in order to hold onto any sense of self, we dreadfully judge everyone else to try to keep the control when we feel so frantically out of control.

When we relate to our Spirit we are able to see the truth that everyone else is pure love too. There's no judgement. We can all breathe a great big sigh of relief!

I love how Robert Holden explains this in his book, 'Loveability':

"The self you judge is not the real self; the self you love is the real you."

I believe that developing a relationship with your Spirit is the most loving thing you could do for yourself. I see so many women really suffering at the hand of judgement. They are crippled by it. It means they are not comfortable in their own skin, let alone in relationship to anyone else. They are so worn down and the guilt they feel on top of the judgement (for being so unkind to themselves and others) is the nail in the coffin.

It doesn't have to be like this!

You ARE beautiful and perfect. So is everyone. And when you get this, you will be free to love and be loved! It is super cool!

Do you know where I love to connect to my Spirit? In the steam room. It is my church! I sit, cocooned in that dark room with its twinkly lights, and I breathe deeply to connect to my truth. I sigh with relief to just be with me and feel so safe and so loved.

You can call on your Spirit at any time. Developing a spiritual practice is a key part of your Self-Love Affair. It could mean meditating, going for a walk, journalling, reading inspirational books, listening to high vibrational music, exercise ... the key is to find what's right for you and mix it up. Enjoy the relationship! Make it fun and make it unique to you.

No matter where you are or what you are doing, your Spirit is always with you. It is you! It is just a choice. You can choose to be guided by your Spirit and let judgement go. You can decide to remember that you are a Spiritual being – not an ego. When you feel the pull or the auto-response to judge (yourself or another), with compassion and kindness simply say to yourself, 'I remember who I am! I choose to see the truth,' and lovingly allow the judgement to fall away. In that moment, allow yourself to feel the power of that statement and feel the connection with who you *really* are.

I believe that the ultimate human endeavour is to achieve enlightenment - something I think only the likes of Jesus and Buddha have demonstrated. I believe that whether we know it or not, that is our purpose. Some are further along that path than others. Just the desire to read a book like this suggests you are on the path because you have an awareness or inner knowing that you are on this planet to be more than just a body at the mercy of fate and you desire to know more. I am a truth seeker too and I research and write and teach about this subject because I desire to understand deeply who I am, who we all are and the impact we have on each other and our world. I think it's exciting!

We are being called! Lady, YOU are being called! It is time to evolve. The human race needs us all to be our best selves - not in terms of being more than or better than anyone else (that is ego-identification) but to drop the fear-based beliefs and behaviours and relationships and to tune into our loving nature. That will serve us individually and collectively. That is what will heal the world.

I believe that the journey towards the ultimate goal of enlightenment means we are assigned the task of learning to identify with our Spirit. Not our ego. We must unlearn our disempowering attachment to fear and learn to lean into love. This is our daily assignment. It is to be practised every single day. It is a muscle to be worked.

We must learn to love ourselves and when we come from Spirit, it is so much easier to do because judgement and criticism and jealousy and competition all fall away. All our fearful ways of thinking and operating are replaced with love.

Love yourself enough to remember the truth of you every single day.

The quickest way to transform your life is to love yourself because when you are at that vibration, literally everything around you shifts!

- - - - -

Remember, resistance is totally normal in the process of change, which is why being kind to yourself is so crucial at this time. You are learning to do life differently. You are choosing to live life from a place of self-love. You have never done this before! There's loads to learn and course correcting to be done. The point is though that you are DOING it! You have begun your journey of transformation. Your trainer wheels are on and you are learning a new way of being. You are discovering that a life rooted in love is far nicer than one rooted in fear.

Love yourself enough to be patient with yourself.

 AN EXERCISE

1. Congratulate yourself!

You have come a long way already and have been working so hard at understanding who you are.

Consider what you could do to honour the work you have done so far. How can you reward or treat yourself?

Whatever you choose to do, remember to be intentional about the celebration and the gift you are giving yourself. I cannot stress enough how important it is to celebrate every step of your Self-Love Affair.

2. Practice the art of receiving!

Start by writing a list of all the things you do for other people. It may astound you how much you do for others and how little you do for yourself or how often you dare to put yourself first!

Consider what on this list you could do for yourself.

Have a think about where in your life you could ask for help and support.

3. Gather evidence!

Write a list of 100 things you love about yourself! If you need help, perhaps ask people you trust what they love about you to add to your list of evidence that you are loveable!

4. Commit to loving your body.

Write the following in your journal: "I choose to love myself and care for my body by...." List at least 20 things you could do to nurture your body.

5. Commit to loving your mind.

Write the following in your journal: "I choose to love myself and care for my mind by...." List at least 20 things you could do to nurture your mind.

6. Commit to loving your inner child.

Write the following in your journal: "I choose to love myself and show my inner child compassion by...." List at least 20 things you could do to nurture your child.

7. Commit to loving your Spirit.

Write the following in your journal: "I choose to love myself and connect to my Spirit by...." List at least 20 things you could do to stay in connection with your Spirit.

I am... YOUR AFFIRMATIONS:

I love myself.

Today I choose to be compassionate towards myself.

I am kind to myself.

I love to give myself permission to ...

I have a choice in all things.

I love to express my emotions.

I remember who I am! I choose to see the truth.

You can say these into the mirror:

I love you.

I see you.

I accept you.

I am here for you.

I understand you.

Thank you!

How can I make you happy today?

What do you desire today?

I forgive you.

 *A MEDITATION*

The Open Heart Visualisation - you can download the audio of this meditation for free at: http://daringandmighty.com/meditation-library

Prepare your meditation space, light a candle and enjoy this beautiful 20-minute visualisation whenever you desire to experience the healing energy of your heart.

 *PUMP UP THE VOLUME:*

"Break the Cycle" - You+Me

"Keep Your Head Up" - Ben Howard

"Lift Me Up" - The Afters

"Paradise" - Coldplay

Connection to Others

"When you meet anyone, remember it is a holy encounter. As you see him, you will see yourself. As you treat him, you will treat yourself. As you think of him, you will think of yourself. Never forget this, for in him you will find yourself or lose yourself." A Course in Miracles

As I tread the Daring & Mighty path, committed to the assignment of loving myself every day, I am continually being shown that our relationship to others is key to the evolution of our soul. The closer the relationship, often the deeper the opportunity for growth. Sometimes, however, a chance and brief encounter with a stranger can be an enormous opportunity too!

This has not been an easy lesson for me and I put my hands up right here, right now, and declare to you that I am very much a student when it comes to developing connection to others. I lean on incredible teachers around this subject - the likes of Brene Brown, Byron Katie, Melody Beattie, Robert Holden, Louise Hay, Sue Minns, Marianne Williamson and 'A Course in Miracles'. Whenever I find myself challenged in relationship - whether that be with a friend, a lover, a relative, my son or a colleague - I will invariably open a book and look for guidance and inspiration. And I pray!

There are no coincidences and I just love how the Universe lined up a perfect mix of support, challenges and lessons in the lead-up to writing this chapter, making it clear to me that I am held supported to write on this subject while very much being a student of it.

I set aside a few days specifically to focus on this piece. By 'chance' I found myself at a Marianne Williamson workshop on the subject of 'Love and Relationships' the day before I was due to begin writing. The day before that workshop I had a very painful encounter with some friends. A few days before that, I had a gloriously joyful encounter with some other friends. Within the same week, my son's school announced that week to be 'friendship week' and I sat in a special assembly listening to children read poems about what the key ingredients are for a good friend – a dollop of love, a spoonful of trust, lashings of kindness – and it was all I could do not to cry at the simplicity of the message.

A couple of days ago I was about to begin my practice of morning journalling and meditation and I *stopped* to flick through my journal to discover these poignant and very relevant words that I had written a few months ago:

> Something massive has awakened inside me.
>
> And I know it is love.
>
> Love to serve and help others. I've never felt it like this before and I feel I could burst.
>
> Love for friends who are now my family.
>
> Love for my life – the adventure of it – the learning and growth.
>
> I feel expanded and enlightened.
>
> I feel free.
>
> I feel whole.
>
> Alight.
>
> Alive.
>
> Awake.
>
> Fucking fabulous!
>
> Creative.
>
> Flowing.
>
> Feminine.
>
> Beautiful.

My Spirit roars – she is free!

I am free.

Me.

I dare to receive.

I am awakened.

I swear I never knew love until now.

Except the day Finn was born.

And today I feel like that again, simply because I've connected with other people.

I've dared to love.

Wow......

Wow indeed!

As I read those words, which I had totally forgotten I'd written, I remembered that day – the absolute ecstasy I felt to feel so much love and connection with others. I remembered that I had given a lot to friends during that period of time and the giving was unconditional and full of love. The unconditional love I gave out came back to me by the bucket load. It wasn't expected and actually it wasn't entirely from those friends – it was more a natural filling-up inside me. As I gave, I received an ability to love myself more. I experienced love as expansive and endless. I witnessed it as being limitless and always available to me. There would always be more than enough. It felt miraculous.

Needless to say that as I flicked through my journal entries after that day, all sorts of incredible and miraculous things were transpiring in my life. Such is the power of connection!

Why?

Because to believe we are fundamentally disconnected from others causes pain. To think we are alone and having to tough out this life on our own puts us in a very low vibration indeed. When we remember that we are energetic beings and as such, connected to every thing and every person, we can breathe. We are connected. It is law. To deny that is to deny ourselves. To try and do life alone means pushing against a principle that is fundamental to our very existence and our survival. (Remember the six human needs? Love and connection are a requirement for survival.)

We are spiritual beings. We are 100% delicious, beautifully perfect, eternal love. We are connected. Fact! It is our choice whether to connect through the vehicle of fear or love.

I know only too well the feeling of connection through fear. It is ugly and it is literally soul destroying. Connection through love lifts us up. It lifts our Spirit. From that place, we are magnetic and we attract wondrous things into our lives.

Connection through fear looks like this - jealousy, judgement, worry, dependency, anxiety, blame, fighting, betrayal, denial, pain, distrust, need to be right, emotional repression, disappointment, craziness, miscommunication, anger, hostility, competition, obsession, control, guilt, war.....you get the idea.

When we relate to others from the place of ego, we relate in fear.

When we relate to others from the place of Spirit, we relate in love.

Connection through love means we make the decision to see every other person as a spiritual being doing his or her best in this lifetime. I learned a beautiful tool from Marianne Williamson and that is to spend at least a couple of minutes every day honouring the love and light in other people. As I walk though the tube station or around the supermarket I look at the strangers' faces around me and I repeat these words in my head: *"The love in me salutes the love in you," "The light in me salutes the light in you."* It dissolves fear instantly and I see each individual as a perfect being of love. As I do this, I feel full with love. With every blessing I send out, I too am blessed. It feels so good! When I sit in meditation in the morning, I am able to envisage the faces of any 'challenging' people in my life and offer them the same words. It allows me to see them as innocent children, simply desiring to be unconditionally loved. It takes the pain away. It softens me and my attitude towards them and the fear-based situation. Then I ask for a miracle – that fear is removed and I see them with love. It's a beautiful practice.

In the same way that self-love requires you to offer yourself compassion, understanding, self-care and connection, that is what must be offered to others in order to connect through love.

Connection with others is an assignment in learning to be vulnerable because it means dropping the ego and enlisting your heart to do the work. This requires huge amounts of strength and bravery. Being vulnerable leaves you wide open and the ego absolutely hates that! You will be challenged enormously when you choose to open your heart and allow others to see the real you. It could mean that some people leave your life and that can be so painful. It will mean wonderful new people come into your life too!

You know how exhausting it is to keep up appearances! Vulnerability allows you to let that go and just be you. It means you are able to surround yourself with people who support who you authentically are. Indeed, it means your life is filled with people who celebrate you for being you. You lift each other up! What a joy that is!

As you strengthen your self-love muscle, you will start to know deeply that you are enough and that you are worthy of the love of others and of giving love to others. It also helps you to develop strong healthy boundaries that ensure you are only surrounded by people who lift you higher while allowing the others to naturally fall away and offering them the blessing that they too discover a connection with the truth that they are love.

"Your capacity to love yourself also influences how much you let yourself be loved by others." Robert Holden (Loveability)

I personally find vulnerability in an intimate relationship the hardest of all. My background and conditioning has meant I have always found it hard to trust a man. Intimacy has always frightened me because I have always been so fearful of being let down or left. Being vulnerable meant being imperfect and the fear was that when they discovered my imperfections, they would run a mile!

My pattern was to claim approval and worthiness from a man. If he left me, the fear was that I would become nothing. It would prove my worthlessness and unloveability. I would cease to exist (or at least that's how it felt).

My journey to self-love has meant that I am able to find my worthiness and approval from myself - not from anything outside of me. I have come a long, long way and I am still a student when it comes to releasing co-dependent patterns and surrendering into vulnerability with a man. As I write this I am single but I am lifted by the very solid men I have found coming my way that reflect back to me that I am now a woman who loves, trusts and honours herself - because the men I meet offer that to themselves and to me.

As I venture out into the world of dating (after several years of choosing to be single and having a Self-Love Affair!), I am reassured by a strong feeling that because I love myself, if a man was to 'reject' me, I am internally strong enough to handle it. I will feel the pain, of course, but I will not feel as if my world is going to crash down around me. I will not feel damaged and as if there is something terribly wrong with me. With self-love I have developed a deep belief that I am worthy of love so when the right person comes along, I will be ready and able to receive it and give it.

I have been told that when I am vulnerable, I am easier to love. That there is beauty in my vulnerability. That I don't have to be perfect. I can just be real. Now isn't that a lovely breath of fresh air!

"Relationships are assignments. They are part of a vast plan for our enlightenment, the Holy Spirit's blueprint by which each individual soul is led to greater awareness and expanded love. Relationships are the Holy Spirit's laboratories in which He brings together people who have the maximal opportunity for mutual growth."
Marianne Williamson (A Return to Love)

As you have discovered, healing ourselves through a process of honest self-awareness, emotional expression and forgiveness is a path to self-love.

Connecting to others is the other path to healing. They do not stand separate and there isn't a choice between one or the other. Both are required and like anything, the deeper you throw yourself into the assignment, the more you will get out of it.

Relationships with others are an opportunity to know ourselves more deeply and an awesome opportunity to deepen our healing. As with our personal process of self actualisation, the key to healing within relationship is honesty. In the same way that you have needed to be brutally honest with yourself during phase one of your Self-Love Affair, it's equally important to relate from a place of real honesty with other people. That vulnerability will be the key to an incredible opportunity for your soul's growth.

It's all very well healing on your own. Allowing someone else to be a part of that process takes the challenge to a whole other level because you are allowing someone else to see you, warts 'n' all!

You have probably heard it said that relationships are a mirror. What is being presented to you by another person is actually a reflection of your inner world. It's a gift of insight that you may not have been able to see on your own. When someone is angry with you there is an opportunity for you to look within and understand what unresolved anger you are harbouring towards yourself or others. If someone seemingly disrespects you, you can ask yourself how respectful you are being to yourself or others. If you find yourself amidst a whole lot of drama you've got to ask the question, where is there drama in me that needs resolution? If you find yourself not trusting someone, could it be that you don't trust yourself? Or if you are feeling judged, are you guilty of judging yourself and/or others? If someone makes it clear that you are not up to their standard - that you are not good enough - then it allows you to question if you think *you* are good enough.

Naturally, that mirror is often a projection of what is going on for the other person too. If anger, disrespect, drama, distrust, judgement and so on are being shown towards you, not only is that a sign of what could be going on in your internal world, it is also likely to be what is going on internally for that person too. They project their 'stuff' in your direction because for whatever reason, you have made yourself available to receive it - whether that be consciously or unconsciously. Energetically, you have attracted that person into your life because there is something within you being offered up for transformation. Your availability can be your opportunity for healing and that healing could come in the form of consciously working through your 'stuff' within that relationship or setting a healthy boundary around it (a little more on that later) or perhaps consciously choosing someone else to help you heal that part of you - perhaps a counsellor or coach or psychotherapist. The choice is yours.

Like attracts like, so it is often the case that two people will come together with similar 'stuff' to heal, whether that's within an intimate relationship, friendship, relative or co-worker. As I said, I am single but that doesn't mean I escape opportunities for growth from my relationship to certain others! Intimate relationship does, however, provide a very intense melting pot for healing should both parties consent to the ride!

The same principles apply in the positive. If you attract an intimate partner who feels honourable and trustworthy, it is likely a reflection that you honour and trust yourself. Perhaps you also desire to honour and trust yourself even more deeply – so you are making yourself available to be taught that by example. If you find yourself surrounded by friends who celebrate you then you are likely very good at celebrating yourself and others and perhaps desire to get even better at it. If you enjoy great company then you very likely enjoy relaxing in your own company. Caring for others allows you to care more deeply for yourself. Being kind to others means you are bringing wonderful kind energy into your own life.

This idea relates to situations as well as people. For example, if you approach a situation in anger, you can rest assured you will be met with anger in return – maybe not from the same person or within the same moment, but anger will come back at you, and it could be an internal attack. If you have peace within, it is likely you will be met with peace and enjoy a calm existence. What we give out is what we get back. If you are lacking something in your life then you are probably not giving it. It ties in with one of the Seven Spiritual Laws – The Law of Giving – which basically states that we will enjoy an abundant and love-filled life when we are willing to give what we desire to seek.

We can understand a lot about ourselves by what is going on around us and the people that come in and out of our life. That is why our connection to other people is such a powerful opportunity to deepen our self-knowing. There is only so much we can see for ourselves. Allowing another to shine a light on our wounds speeds up our healing.

Equally, being vulnerably available to others means making yourself available to enable their healing too. I know that the way I persist with my own healing helps those closest to me. My son witnesses me living consciously, intending to do life from a place of love rather than fear. My friends and family also witness me doing this. Taking responsibility for my life can only inspire others to do the same. If I am always questioning how I can 'be love' in a situation, then that offers them an opportunity to reflect and ask themselves how are they showing up in the world too.

I know that the nature of my relationships is reflective of my own internal state. So the more I stay in tune with me, the more harmonious my relationships will be.

The Universe perfectly aligns us with people who will reflect back to us what we need to learn. The most difficult relationships can teach us the most. Simple relationships make the ride easier but they are not the opportunity for growth that a relationship fraught with fear can offer.

The trick then is to assess if the relationship is appropriate in terms of personal growth or an opportunity to create a healthy boundary. Self-love means trusting your intuition. What does your Spirit whisper to you? Is that person a challenge that will lead you closer to enlightenment or is that person a chance to demonstrate the resolve of your self-worth? The assignment is for you to decipher – to go with it or to distance it from your life. The only way to know is to develop that relationship with your Spirit and trust yourself. That 'knowing' may take a little practice and it is very much about learning to tune into God's voice and tune out from the voice of ego. As you know, the more we identify with our ego, the more fear we experience. The key is to identify with our Spirit and get into the habit of prayer as a way of communicating with our inner voice. As that relationship strengthens, our ability to choose the people we relate to becomes much easier.

For me, a key way to understand if I desire to learn from a relationship or to remove myself from it altogether lies within that person's willingness to evolve too. If their heart is open to the challenge that this relationship presents, that tells me we both have an opportunity to grow together. If my instinct tells me that person is not on the path of enlightenment, then perhaps it would be better for me to remove myself from that situation. The truth is some are further along the path of self-actualisation than others.

Another way I decipher whether a relationship is right for me is to ask myself if I am willing to be part of their growth too. It's not all about me, after all! Do I love them enough to allow them to be vulnerably themselves? Do I desire their full potential to be realised and am I willing to be part of that journey - both the highs and the lows?

Remember, you always have a choice. You are allowed to choose how long you remain in a particular type of relationship. You can choose to experience your lessons through joy or through pain. As I said earlier, you also have the choice of hiring a professional to assist your healing, which can sometimes be the healthiest and fastest route to deep and lasting transformation. That was certainly my experience.

You can also trust that the Universe will never stop presenting you with a lesson you need to learn. You can deny the opportunity over and over and it will continue to be presented. When you are ready, you can accept the challenge.

"Forgiveness takes away what stands between your brother and yourself."
A Course in Miracles

When presented with an opportunity to choose to continue with any type of relationship or not, I see it as an opportunity to explore compassion and acceptance for that person. I know I must offer this to myself if I am going to love myself. So too must I offer this to people that come into my life - whether it's a chance encounter with a stranger for a few moments in a coffee shop or a long term intimate relationship.

I am not saying this is easy, by the way. I find this a challenge and it is a muscle I work on every single day!!

The truth is we are all vulnerable children at heart. We all just want to be loved and accepted and heard and seen. The way we go about getting that can repel people. Often behaviour that is rooted in fear is a cry for love and acceptance. Before I allow my ego to step in and judge, my assignment is to give the benefit of the doubt and offer compassion and acceptance to that person as a fellow Spirit. They are more likely to heal if I view them with a forgiving heart. Holding them up to the light might be the chance they needed to wake up to their truth. And as I do that, it awakens me to my infinite capacity to love, because we are all love.

My mum taught me to 'do unto others as I would have them do unto me'. It's pretty simple really and it's another of the Seven Spiritual Laws – The Law of Karma – which means that the way we treat others will be our experience of life.

So treat others as you would like to be treated! For me that means asking what I could offer someone in terms of lifting them up and holding them in the light. It could be a compliment, encouragement, humour, lightheartedness, an open-hearted conversation with compassionate ears or simply allowing them in front of me in a queue. If I offer love, generosity and happiness, then that will be my experience of life too.

At this point I would like to offer a word of warning to you if you have a tendency to be co-dependent to any degree. In her book, 'Co-dependent No More', Melody Beattie defines a co-dependent as 'one who has let another person's behaviour affect him or her, and who is obsessed with controlling that person's behaviour'.

'Doing unto others' is meant to feel easy and graceful. It is done from a place of free will and unconditional love. Not from guilt, fear, lack, worry or shame. When you love yourself, you are committed to yourself first. Indeed, you are no good to anyone else unless you can put yourself, your feelings, your needs and your desires first. When you love yourself you honour, trust and respect yourself. You are loyal to yourself! From that place you are able to truly be of service to others. Pleasing others, putting everyone else's needs before your own, always saying yes and over-committing yourself is exhausting and it suggests a need for approval from others because an internal lack of self-approval is running the show.

I love what Melodie Beattie says in 'Codependent No More':

"I believe God wants us to help people and share our time, talents, and money. But I also believe He wants us to give from a position of high self-esteem. I believe acts of kindness are not kind unless we feel good about ourselves, what we are doing, and the person we are doing it for. I think God is in each of us and speaks to each of us. If we absolutely can't feel good about something we're doing, then we shouldn't do it – no matter how charitable it seems. We also shouldn't do things for others that they ought to and are capable of doing for themselves. Other people aren't helpless. Neither are we."

So when it comes to connecting with others and honouring the Spiritual Law of Karma, I would like to share the following truths with you, as defined by me:

You are not responsible for anyone else's feelings and it's safe to feel your own.

You are not responsible for what anyone else thinks and you are capable of making decisions and having your own opinion.

You are not responsible for anyone else's desires and you are filled with dreams of your own that you deserve.

You are not responsible for fixing or rescuing anyone else and you are capable of healing yourself.

You are not responsible for caring for anyone else and you are worthy of giving yourself what you need.

You are not responsible for anyone else's happiness and it is your right to create your own happiness.

You are not responsible for anyone else's life and you are capable and trustworthy enough to be able to depend on yourself.

You can't change or control anyone else – you can only do that for yourself and lead by example. Be the light to others and let it be their choice to be inspired by you or not.

Putting yourself first does not mean you do not care for anyone else.

Actually, ultimately the opposite is true! When you love and care for yourself you can love and care for others in such a beautiful way! They benefit from getting the very best of you!

My favourite mantras when I feel myself succumb to any level of co-dependent behaviour are:

"Mind your own business!"

"It's ok to say no!"

"I receive with ease and grace."

"I approve of me. I know I am worthy and more than enough!"

Remember, you exist and are here for a reason. Just being you is enough!

We all exist to evolve and expand as spiritual beings. We are all just doing our best with the tools we have been given. When we remember that we are all connected, it makes sense that what we put out is going to come back. How we treat others is a sign of how we treat ourselves.

Loving yourself requires you to connect to others through love. To what extent you invite any person into your life is your choice, but know this: within that choice lies an opportunity for you to know yourself more deeply and love yourself more fiercely.

 *EXERCISES:*

1. Random acts of kindness

Every day this week why not offer someone an act of goodwill? It could be smiling at a stranger, helping someone with their shopping, having a cup of tea with an elderly neighbour, sending an anonymous gift to someone you know needs a lift, paying for a parking space and leaving the receipt for someone else to use, telling the bank clerk she is doing a great job today....you get the drift. Give out kindness and watch how it transforms how you feel and what you attract into your day as a result! If you dare, extend this to a 21-day commitment and allow yourself to create a brand new habit of behaviour!

2. Clearing Conversations

Nearly everyone has at least one relationship in their life they desire to be transformed. No doubt on the back of all the work you have done so far you may even want to heal a relationship with your mum or dad – perhaps offer up forgiveness and ask for forgiveness in return if that feels right for you. If there is someone in your life with whom you desire to connect more deeply – and if it feels safe to do so – why not commit to having a healing conversation with them. Prepare yourself for the conversation first. Journal around the purpose of the conversation and what you would like to say. Get clear on how you would like to feel while having the conversation and how you would like both of you to feel at the end. Plan when and where you will have this conversation to ensure you will both feel safe enough to be open, honest and vulnerable. Before the conversation, intentionally open your heart. Tune into your Spirit and ask that you speak your truth in love. See the other person as a small innocent child who, just like you, is doing his/her best to live life with the tools they have been given. Enter the conversation without any expectation from the other person. Allow them their feelings and their response and remember you are not responsible for their happiness.

3. Prayer

Do you have a relationship that needs healing but for whatever reason, you feel a clearing conversation is not possible at the moment? If you do, begin a practice of intentional prayer around that situation. If you could have figured out the situation on your own you would have done so by now, so it's time to ask for a miracle. It's time to lean on God. Invite a miracle into your life and set the intention to be available to recognise it and receive it graciously when it arrives. Perhaps create a ritual around your daily prayer. Light a candle and say your prayer out loud. Something along the lines of, "I am upset and angry but I am willing not to be. I am willing to see him/her as an innocent Spirit who is doing his/her best in this world. I am willing to forgive us both for the roles we have played. I am available for a miracle!" Watch what happens over the coming days / weeks and expect a miracle!

I am... YOUR AFFIRMATIONS

I mind my own business.

I can say no.

I receive with ease and grace.

I am worthy and more than enough.

I have healthy, healing, joyful relationships.

I have a choice in all things.

I can connect to others through love.

It is safe for me to be vulnerable.

I attract where I am at.

I can trust my inner voice.

I treat others as I treat myself.

I can put myself first.

PUMP UP THE VOLUME:

"Nothing's Real But Love" - Rebecca Ferguson

"I Want Your Love" - Transvision Vamp

"Love" - American Authors

"Love Now" - Calvin Harris, All About She

"Real Love" - Tom Odell

"We Found Love" - Calvin Harris, Rihanna

"Skinny Love" - Birdy

"Make You Feel My Love" - Adele

"You've Got The Love" - Florence + The Machine

"This Love" - Maroon 5

"True Love" - Coldplay

"This Year's Love" - David Gray

"Could You Be Loved" - Bob Marley & The Wailers

"Goodbye My Lover" - James Blunt

"Love Is Easy" - McFly

"You Can't Hurry Love" - The Supremes

"I Will Always Love You" - Whitney Houston

"Higher Love" - James Vincent McMorrow

"Love Shack" - The B52s

"Fight For This Love" - Cheryl

"It Must Have Been Love" - Roxette

"Sowing The Seeds Of Love" - Tears For Fears

"To Be Loved" - Michael Buble

"Crazy Little Thing Called Love" - Queen

PART 3: MY VISION. MY FUTURE.

"When I get lonely these days, I think: So BE lonely, Liz. Learn your way around loneliness. Make a map of it. Sit with it, for once in your life. Welcome to the human experience. But never again use another person's body or emotions as a scratching post for your own unfulfilled yearnings."
Elizabeth Gilbert, 'Eat, Pray, Love'

I love the quote above. It's such a strong statement of responsibility.

Only you are responsible for your life. Only you can feel your feelings. Only you can transform your beliefs. Only you can find yourself. Only you can create your future.

I will put my hand up and admit that many, many times in my life I have looked to someone or something else to be my happiness. I have expected someone else to create a life for me. I have looked to all sorts of things outside of me for fulfilment.

The truth is, the buck stops with me.

The other truth is the Universe has eyes! When I step up and take responsibility for myself and my life, I am supported 100%!

You have created huge awareness around the truth of who you are and witnessed yourself as a magnificent Spirit connected to all others through love. You have given yourself permission to love and honour yourself.

You know who you are.

Now it's time to discover what you value and desire. When you are crystal clear on that, the Universe will know how to guide and support you.

Your work now is to focus all that you are, all that you value and all that you desire into creating a life that feels magical and joyful. It's time for you to connect to your passion and your purpose and allow the creative intelligence that is source energy to manifest your dreams.

You are a Daring & Mighty Super Hero! The way you do life is now your choice. It's your story to create and it can be on-demand, in high definition 3D with surround sound!

Because you know you are worth it!

PUMP UP THE VOLUME:

"Live Louder" - Nathaniel

What Do You Value?

"Hell is the opposite of joy. It is unfulfillment. It is knowing Who and What You Are, and failing to experience that. It is being less. That is hell, and there is none greater for your soul." Neal Donald Walsh

I absolutely love the quote above from the book, 'Conversations with God'. To know your Spirit is to remember the truth of you. Once you have remembered who you are, your purpose is to express that. If you do not, if you choose to be *less* than you are, you are not allowing your soul to experience joy, which is its driving force.

If you have read to this point and have done all the exercises set then you have been digging really deep into the truth of you. You have begun the process of stripping out the pieces that do not serve you and you have been healing your wounds with the divine assistance of your S-Team. You have been developing compassion, understanding and unconditional love for all parts of yourself - your Spirit, your mind, your body and your inner child. You are becoming your own best friend and, from that place, are learning how to relate to others in a healthy, open-hearted and compassionate way.

I wonder how you are feeling right now?

I hope you are proud of the work you have done. Your commitment to yourself and your life is certainly something to be proud of!

Are you ready for more?! Are you ready to take it to the next level?!

Yes? Awesome! Let's do this!

I bet you are ready to begin the process of creating a life you are proud of. I bet your Spirit is chomping at the bit to get cracking with living out your purpose. To show up in the world as your divine, authentic, stupendous self. Because that is what you are here to do.

You are ready!

In order to get clarity on all that you desire to have and create, it's essential to get clear on what you value. When you know what you value, you can create a set of what I like to call 'Life Rules'. That will allow you to create a life that is 100% in alignment with the truth of you and all you stand for.

You have discovered the truth that you are worthy and meant to be here. The depth to which you believe you are worthy is the extent to which you are able to add real value to your life.

It's time to get really specific around what it is in life that is worthy of your time, energy and attention. What it is that will have you feeling beautifully fulfilled.

Once you are clear on your values you will find it so much easier to make decisions because you have a crib sheet to check against to ensure you are honouring your worth.

Let's say you are offered a full time job that offers a great salary with great benefits. It's a one hour commute from home and you are wondering whether or not to take it. You can take a look at your values and assess which will get a tick if you accept the offer. You may place a high value on financial security so that box gets ticked because the salary offers you that security. If you also place a high value on your family life and being available to collect your children from school each day then that box wouldn't be ticked because the full time hours and commute would make that impossible. If you also have high values around freedom and exercise you may not feel able to tick those boxes because a full time position working for someone else makes you feel trapped and the set hours mean you would have to give up your beloved Friday morning yoga class. So, although the financial security sounds great and makes the opportunity seem really enticing, the fact that you are not able to tick a significant number of your values boxes makes your decision an easy no. You are then available to explore options that are more fully in alignment with all that you value, not to mention the fact that holding such clear intention around your values will turn you into a magnet to attract perfect, value-fulfilling opportunities! (But more on that later....!)

Your values will be completely unique to you. The way you desire to do life will very likely be different to everyone else. When you create your values you get to honour your unique and quirky likes and dislikes and you can identify values that support how you desire to feel. You can choose to have people in your life who are aligned to your truth. You can choose to live in an environment that is reflective of you. It's your life, after all! This is a chance for you to give yourself permission to design a life that is all about you. You are no longer a puppet to someone else's conditioning and you no longer care what anyone else thinks about your choices.

How would it feel to make decisions based on what lights YOU up? Decisions that are not linked to keeping up appearances or making Mum or Dad proud? Decisions that are fueled by beliefs that are loving and that serve you? Decisions that make you feel good? We make choices all day, every day. When you have your values written down, that process becomes so much more simple and joyful.

It's time to claim you and your life back.

Here are some examples of core values to get those cogs moving...!

Adventure	Alone Time
Achievement	Beauty
Challenge	Charity
Creativity	Community
Comfort	Commitment

Courage	Education
Empowerment	Environment
Entertainment	Family
Financial Freedom	Fitness
Freedom	Friendship
Health	Intelligence
Independence	Inner Peace
Inspiration	Intimacy
Joy	Leadership
Luxury	Lifestyle
Learning	Love
Motivation	Optimism
Passion	Personal Growth
Play	Respect
Relationship	Reliability
Security	Service
Success	Self-Care
Self-Love	Strength
Support	Spirituality
Time	Travel
Trust	Wealth

 *AN EXERCISE*

Answer the following questions:

1. How do you fill your space? What do you surround yourself with at home and/or work?

2. What is your favourite book or film or stage play? What values are being represented?

3. How do you spend your money? Have a think about your bank statement - what comes up as the most regular expenses?

4. How do you spend your time? What do you always have time for?

5. How do you use your energy? What activities make you feel more energised?

6. Where are you most organised in your life? In what areas of your life are you tidy and ordered?

7. Where are you most reliable in your life? Where do you have the most discipline and focus? What things do you never have to be reminded to do because you are driven internally to do them?

8. What do you spend time dreaming about? What does your heart yearn for?

9. What do you talk about to your friends? What topics of conversation do you bring up in social situations? What topics make you feel instantly excited, chatty and confident?

10. What inspires you? What have you done in the past that has inspired you? Which people inspire you? What do they do? What do they have in common?

11. What do you love to learn and read about the most?

12. Think back to some very memorable, happy days of your life. Which values were being ticked?

13. Think of a time when things felt hard and you were miserable or scared or lost. Which values were not being ticked?

When you have answered all of these questions, take a look at all the values you have listed. Are there any that don't feel true for you anymore? You have answered these questions based on your life up to this moment. Your life before you discovered many of your beliefs and behaviours were not actually yours. It's possible that how you have been spending your time, money and energy up to this moment isn't 100% reflective of the woman you desire to be. So which values are listed that you no longer want? Cross them out and consider what you would like instead. If you desire to replace that value with something more loving and in service to the life you are creating, add that value to your list the same number of times as the old value featured.

Next, take a look at which values repeat the most regularly. Rate them in order of how frequently they come up. Your highest value will feature the most often. Aim to have between 10 and 15 values in total and write them as a list in order of most often featured down to least often featured.

This list is your highest core values.

Congratulations! How does it feel to have identified what truly lights you up and to have a measure by which to make decisions in all areas of your life?

Would you like to take this one step further and ramp up your list another notch? You are Daring & Mighty, after all!

Ask yourself if there is anything not showing up in your life that you really desire. Then take a look to see if that features on your list of core values. If it doesn't, add it to your list. Remember, this isn't an exact science and there is no right or wrong. So if you feel that something significant is missing from your list, add it on! Also remember that this list is your HIGHEST values. You will have many, many more than feature here. The point of this exercise is to create your absolute non-negotiable priorities when it comes to designing your life.

When I did this exercise a few years ago, I discovered that money didn't feature on my list in any way and yet I was skint and deeply desired the security that financial freedom would give me. I was fearful of money and had a money story that kept me stuck in struggle, worry, stress and anxiety. I avoided thinking about money as much as possible because it filled me with dread and panic. My assignment was to add Financial Security to the very top of my list of values and then do the work to transform my fear-based beliefs around money to beliefs that had me feeling excited, alive and optimistic when I thought of money. (I will share with you how I did that shortly.)

As you know, as a spiritual being you are always expanding and evolving so naturally your values will shift as you up-level your life. It is important to check in and consider re-writing your values and re-assessing your life at regular intervals. When you are experiencing great personal growth in life, you will probably find you need to update your values more regularly. My values have shifted significantly every six months for the last few years. The top value on my list alone has changed four times in the last couple of years, from my son to financial security to romantic relationship to business support. Once upon a time inner peace and self-care didn't feature on my list but they do now and some values have remained very firmly unchanged – trust, friendship, family, spirituality, travel, creativity, inspiration and time.

Getting so crystal clear on your values means you have essentially placed your order with the Universe around what you expect from now on. You are now laser focussed on your value and what is worthy of your energy. That focus is very, very powerful (and you will discover why in a later chapter).

When you look at your list, ask yourself if the way you are spending your money, using your time, choosing your friends, focussing your energy and attention is in alignment with your values. It is up to you now to begin to re-align your behaviour with what you value. As you do this, be kind to yourself. Remember that you love yourself and offer yourself understanding and compassion as you forge new behavioural patterns. And enjoy the ride!

Now that you have identified your top non-negotiables in life you can create your Life Rules! This is a chance for you to get creative and rather daring. Based on your values list, how do you choose to do life? I will share with you some of my rules to get you thinking – and this is by no means the entire list!

1. I love myself, unconditionally.

2. I honour my Spirit and nurture myself with activities that feed my soul.

3. My son has the best of me. Always.

4. I am a student of life. Learning something new every day means I am growing and being inspired.

5. My work is my joy and inspiration. I am designed to work with passion and balance.

6. Time out creates time.

7. I expect financial abundance because I know there is a limitless supply for all. Financial freedom allows me to support my highest values.

8. I love to travel so I plan at least 10 trips a year that involve getting on a plane! An injection of new cultures, languages and food is soul-nourishing.

9. I plan get-togethers with friends and family. I am even brave enough to cook for them! I love to entertain and I love to be

surrounded by the energy of high-vibrational people.

10. I plan time away with my gal pals!

11. I listen to inspired thought. I take hints from the Universe. I take action.

12. I start my day with an intention.

13. I choose every day to accept where I am. To feel my emotions, knowing that passing through them means getting to the other side. The other side is an evolved, fully present, higher-vibrational me.

14. I choose every day to create a life I love. I know my thoughts today are my experience tomorrow.

15. I keep a gratitude and success journal.

16. I have a massage once a month.

17. I have a cleaner.

18. I am well supported in my business and am surrounded by high-vibrational, expert colleagues.

19. I live by the sea.

20. I eat well and respect what I put into my body.

21. I meditate regularly and am committed to my spiritual practices.

22. I create time for fun and mischief!

Now it's time for you to go ahead and write your rules for life! Get excited! It's time to break the rules others set for you. What rules do you want to live by? And remember, your rules will give you freedom to live a life you love!

I encourage you to stick your list of Core Values and Life Rules somewhere where you can read them regularly. Memorise them! Fall in love with them. Live by them!

As you embark on living life by your values and your rules it will be very normal to feel challenged at times. Sticking to your guns and honouring your values will take practice because you are learning a new way of doing life and that means transforming any limiting beliefs that tempt you back to the old, seemingly easier way of doing life. Those limiting beliefs have become your story and you are well rehearsed at telling it. Your assignment is to re-write your story.

Let's say you are in the habit of making sure everyone else is ok and have no idea how to put yourself first. Your story could be that others are more worthy than you and more deserving of your attention. If you have added a new value of health/fitness to your list and perhaps a new rule that you will visit the gym three times a week then you will be challenged to write a new story around your deservedness of that routine.

You may have identified this story when doing the work to explore your childhood conditioning. You will have expressed your feelings around the limiting beliefs and offered up forgiveness to all involved and that will have shifted the energy of the belief and transformed your attachment to it significantly. That said, a belief as deep as 'I am not worthy' or 'I am not deserving' is likely to need continued work. Not to mention you are very likely to have attracted people into your life who play a 'supporting role' in your story and who may very well be reminding you of your old script because it's the only one they know how to identify with. When you start speaking new lines, they may not know how to respond and their reaction could be to get angry or frustrated or upset with you, which is painful for everyone. Such emotionally charged interactions questioning your desired new belief or value could send you into a spin and have you wanting to retreat to a comfort zone.

You are Daring & Mighty. Retreat is not an option!

Instead you will stop and feel into the situation and take inspired action. You might line up a clearing conversation. Perhaps you will commit to a ritual of prayer. You may feel the need to write an angry letter and then burn it, followed by an offering of forgiveness. Maybe you choose to do it all! So far, throughout this book you have learned all sorts of tools you could employ at this point.

Creating new beliefs requires dogged determination. It is a muscle to be worked.

I encourage you to commit to yourself with real ferocity. This stuff works when you are absolutely determined to claim a life that you really love!

 *AN EXERCISE*

When an old story comes up, another really great tool to counteract it, get you back to your truth and feel empowered to identify with your desired new story is to write a list of all the things you are telling yourself that are keeping you out of alignment with the values or rules you have created.

Once you have your list of reasons why you can't or shouldn't have what you really desire, write the opposite statement next to each line. Make that statement an affirmation so have it start with words such as 'I am' or 'I have' or 'I love' or 'I create' or 'I can' or 'I will' or 'I choose' or 'I enjoy'.

Connect to the truth that you are a perfect Spirit looking to be the most expanded and loving version of yourself. Look at the two lists. The first will be fear-based thinking that is restricting your beautiful Spirit. The second will be love-based truths that allow your Spirit to soar free.

Notice that the fear-based stories are not you. They are beliefs that perhaps you heard someone say once when you were a child or rules that someone else lived by and modelled to you as the only way to do life.

Notice how the love-based stories make you *feel* instead!

Tear up the old story. Literally! Shred it, stamp on it and burn it. You are done with it and ready to create a new story! Hallelujah!!

Commit to reading and reciting your new affirmations every day. Set them as reminders on your phone with an alarm. Record your voice reading them aloud and listen to the recording on repeat every morning while you get ready for your day. Write them on post-it notes and stick them about the house. Get creative. The key is to have them in your face and in your ears 24/7 until they become part of you.

You can do this with any story. As I was explaining earlier, I did this with my money story and it worked. There are still a few pieces needing work and I am committed to that process of change. Out of the 20 affirmations I created, there are still two or three that need work....they are stubborn little buggers! But I am Daring & Mighty. I WILL transform them!

Whether you have a money story or a love story or a worthiness story or a happiness story, whatever it is, it's within your power to change it.

Go for it!

I am... YOUR AFFIRMATIONS

I am determined to live a life of value.

I am committed to my process of transformation.

I can create new loving stories.

I love to live by my own rules.

PUMP UP THE VOLUME

"Brave" - Sara Bareilles

"What a Life" - Rochelle

"Break the Cycle" - You+Me

Daring Desires!

"Life isn't about finding yourself. Life is about creating yourself."
George Bernard Shaw

Everything you are meant for in this lifetime is guided by your desires.

Our intentions, dreams, ambitions, wishes and hopes are what moves us forward in life. These are our desires and they are a necessary and natural part of life.

The source of our desires is our True Self. Our Spiritual Self. That energy centre which is infinite, unbounded, limitless and fundamental to all creation.

The work we have done so far is to clear the layers of programming and conditioning that have blocked you to your truth. Why? Well, not only does it feel great to operate in life from a place of authenticity and freedom but it also means you are being propelled forward by a purity of purpose. If we are functioning from a conditioned self, our desires are clouded by the inherited desires of others or perhaps in alignment with what we think is expected of us or in response to a story we have told ourselves for years around what is correct or deserving or valid. When we are guided by our True Self, our desires are an absolute reflection of all that we are and who we are meant to be!

When we listen to our desires we can guarantee a life that feels abundant and authentic and free because it is exactly what we were put on the planet to be, do and have. As you now know, to feel happy and fulfilled is your birthright!

When you desire something from a place of truth, you can trust that you are MEANT to have or feel that thing. Your assignment so far has been to remove anything blocking you from claiming your desires. Now your mission is to identify your deepest desires, to open yourself up and give yourself permission to receive them.

A desire is a calling from your Spirit telling you how to express yourself and enjoy this lifetime. When you feel that desire you can know it is already yours because you are part of something so much larger than you. When you are aware of your desires and set the intention to receive them (because now you know you are worthy of them!), source energy will hear your calling and line up all that is required to bring it to you. Sure, some effort and action will be required - and that is covered in the next chapter - but for now, I encourage you to open your heart and your mind to the truth that your desires are MEANT for you and they are the seeds of your purpose.

Your desires are the voice of your Spirit. There is no need to feel worry or guilt or vanity around expressing and claiming them because it is through the receiving of your desires that you get to create joy, love and peace, which has a ripple effect throughout the world.

Imagine if everyone cleared the path to their True Self and lived from a place of authentic desire! The love and fulfillment experienced by every individual would have the most incredible Universal impact.

You are doing the world a disservice not to honour your desires and I encourage you to get as daring as possible in your expression of them! I say daring because we are going for a life of thriving and not one of survival.

The most basic desires of survival are that of your bodily organs. Your heart desires to beat blood around your body. Your lungs desire the exchange of oxygen.

You are moved through your day by basic desires of survival too. You wake up and the desire for food or the loo has you get out of bed. You feel cold so you desire to wear a jumper. You go to work because you desire an income to pay your bills.

You get the idea.

A life of thriving means we are tuned into the desires of our Spirit. As you know, your Spirit's number one desire is to expand and grow. As an energetic being, that is your driving force. Expansion of Spirit looks like joy, light, peace, security, creativity, success, fun, fulfillment and love!

If you are only tuned into desires of survival, life feels dull, flat and grey. Just surviving isn't enough!

If you consciously connect into your desires of thriving, life will become bright, beautiful and exciting!

Remember the chapter earlier where we looked at the six human needs? Do you remember that the first four - certainty, variety, love/connection, significance - were required for basic survival? The last two - contribution and growth - were required for spiritual expansion and hence a feeling of thriving.

To thrive is crucial and just as valid as the desire to survive. There is no either / or. Food in your belly and a roof over your head are just as imperative as honouring your values around travel and beauty, for example.

We women are SO programmed to accepting survival. Giving ourselves permission to have what we desire often feels indulgent and guilty. The truth that I cannot express strongly enough is that there is no need to question your desires and wonder if it's ok to have a massage because surely it would be more sensible to save that money and use it for the heating bill. The truth is there is more than enough available for you. We live in an abundant, miraculous, limitless Universe. There is more than enough money, love, support and time for you. When you claim your desires you are telling the Universe that you know you are worthy of them. You are moving with the flow of life and in alignment with your very nature. By ignoring or repressing or making yourself wrong for your desires you are abandoning the truth of you and going against the laws around which you were created and what you were designed for. When you think and act in a way that goes against your very nature, the Universe is unable to support you. When you dance with the energy of all that you are and trust in the power of all that is, you will be provided for.

The sooner you get on board with this concept, the sooner your life will feel easier. It will take practice and a constant checking in with what you are thinking and how you are behaving to ensure you are in alignment with your truth and not a conditioned story. As you are already discovering, the effort required to become habitually conscious will be well rewarded and honouring your daring desires will become a very natural and normal way of doing life. Indeed, it's the Daring & Mighty way of doing life!

I would like to hazard a guess that the reason you are reading this book is because you desired to love yourself. You desired a deep and true connection with yourself. In other words, you desired a spiritual awakening. Throughout the process of this book you have become conscious of your Spirit and have begun a beautiful relationship with you which is taking you closer and closer to feeling complete and full. As you continue to develop and grow your relationship with your Spirit, your feelings of fulfilment will deepen.

I doubt you will ever stop desiring a deeper connection to your True Self. It is natural to want to focus on your needs for love, compassion, truth and joy because that is the essential nature of your Spirit. When we manifest that feeling of wholeness, everything else in life is so much easier.

I honour your commitment to desiring to know yourself more completely and I want to assure you that this is a desire of the highest calling. You are not weak or damaged or different because of this desire. You are a brave, conscious and magnificently aware creator. You know that life doesn't just happen and that you get to have a choice in its direction through the conscious application of intention.

So what do you desire? In the previous chapter you worked on discovering your values, which has begun the process of having you access your deepest truths. Now let's take a look at what you desire from that authentic place.

What is it that you intend for yourself and your life? What do you choose? How do you want to feel? Where do you want to go? Who do you want to be spending your time with? What do you want to be spending your money on? How do you desire to respond to situations?

Essentially I am taking you back to that chapter very early on in the book where you looked at your life vision and I want you to deepen that vision now. You have gained new self-awareness and you know who you are, why you think and feel the way you do and what you value. Now you can extend your vision and make it even more YOU. Now you get to be your MOST authentic True Self and design a life that totally lights you up.

Now is your time to get really honest with all that you desire and get excited to claim it because remember, if you desire it, it is already yours. If you desire it, your Spirit has informed you that it exists on an energetic level. The next job is to bring it into physical reality (which is the next chapter). The first step, however, is to dream it. From a place of true self-awareness and spiritual connection you are able to see and feel your desires.

So go for it!! What do you desire? What have you been put on this planet to learn, be, do and have?

Look at all your life areas - you know the drill. Check in with yourself and journal on each area of your life. Really go for it!

Not only do I want you to identify what you desire, I also want you to hook into the energy of how you will feel once you have those desires. Get conscious to whether those feelings are in alignment with your spiritual nature.

Do you feel content, loving, safe, compassionate, fulfilled, joyful, creative and nourished? If you do, that's a sure sign the desire is absolutely your truth rather than a construct of your ego.

If the desire has you feel better than someone else or approved of by others, for example, then you know your ego has kicked in so your work is to hook back into the energy of your Spirit and ask what she desires – because only those desires are lasting and truly fulfilling.

The easiest desires to manifest are those that come from your True Self because they have an energy of 'no matter what, I must have this because it is my very nature'. It's almost literally like your life depends on it because, in a way, it really does!

Desires of your Spirit for love, truth, happiness, freedom, beauty, creativity and so forth have you moving closer to feeling whole and complete. You are, of course, already whole and complete; however, your purpose in this lifetime is to get closer to knowing and deeply feeling this truth.

That's not to say that you shouldn't desire material things and in my experience, all sorts of more material desires can absolutely help you to discover the truth of your wholeness. For example, I know that part of the way in which I secured a deep knowing of my worth came through wealth consciousness studies that showed me how to bring more money into my life so I was able to afford all sorts wonderful goodies that which totally light me up! Money was part of the route to me realising my worth and the deeper my self-worth became, the easier it was to manifest money. The key point to note, however, is that I started from a place of desiring to know and love myself rather than simply a desire for more money and 'stuff'. The stuff I spend my money on are things that honour me and are a reflection of who I am and I feel so proud to be able to do that for myself.

My desire for freedom (one of my highest values) had me manifest luxurious holidays, upper class travel and inspirational business trips around the world.

My desire for creativity had me dabble with producing artwork, which turned into a business selling a range of products featuring my affirmation word art designs.

My desire for inspiration and personal growth had me invest in coaches to support me in launching a business that is my purpose and passion.

My desire for friendship and connection had me open my heart to people in a way I never before thought possible and experience love in a way that brings tears to my eyes when I think how blessed I am now with friends that are now my family.

My desire to feel proud of myself has put a fire in my belly to never ever give up on listening to my soul's desire.

My desires were so strong that the Universe supported me in manifesting the money, time and support I needed to make them happen. When I lived from a place of lack and without understanding Universal laws and my oneness with source energy, I would never have believed I could have found the money for a world class coach or the time to travel luxuriously or the support to run a thriving business while being a single parent. As I opened up to my desires and set the intention to be available to receive them, the Universe took over and my life has been truly miraculous.

This is what I desire for you too. And if you are having any doubts let me remind you, I am no different to you and living a miraculous life is available to you too. In fact, when you start living life in this way you will start to see it not as miraculous but as how it was always meant to be. It's totally normal!

When I tap into my desires I feel such power inside me, I tingle and feel expanded. That power is the creative energy that fuels all of life and to feel it within me is just incredible. I am reminded that I am just as powerful as that which keeps the planets in alignment, the sun shining and the plants growing.

You are not separate to the energy that spins our planet! That energy is within you. It surrounds you. And it connects you to every single thing. Your assignment is to tap into that power and live your biggest life.

I encourage you right now to open yourself up to co-creating your life with the Universe. Take a deep breath and allow the energy within you to rise up. Really feel that power within and know that your desires fuel that power.

Remember, a desire is an intention. So what do you intend?

 *MEDITATION*

The True-Self Visualisation – you can download the audio of this meditation for free at: http://daringandmighty.com/meditation-library

Please do the True Self meditation again. Being close to your True Self is the key to staying connected to your deepest, most authentic desires. Your desires are not separate to you. They are fundamentally who you are so staying connected to your Spiritual Self means you stay connected to your desires and are less likely to meet obstacles of the ego that could block you from receiving all you are meant for. Remember, you are worthy and you are enough. When you feel less than that, you are disconnected from your True Self. Remaining in constant connection with the perfect and powerful truth of you means attracting your desires is so easy because the Universe is designed to support the ongoing creation of you! As you will discover in the next chapter, you get what you focus on in life. When you are focussed on the truth that you are whole, complete, worthy and enough the Universe is able to bring you more. You are not focussed on the ego's construct of what you lack so you do not attract lack. You are focussed on the truth that you are fulfilled with light, love and joy and that is what you will attract.

Essentially, who you are is what you become more of so your assignment is to be more and more of you every single day – which is rather exciting, don't you think!?

The Blue Sky Visualisation – you can download the audio of this meditation for free at: http://daringandmighty.com/meditation-library

This is a 15-minute guided visualisation to connect you to your deepest desires! I like to call it a blue sky vision because when we set goals it's important to remember we are not limited in any way. The Universe is abundant and limitless and wants nothing more than to support us in having our greatest dreams become our reality. So why not dream big! This meditation allows you to do just that.

 *EXERCISES*

RECEIVE!

I want you to consciously release anything blocking you to receiving your daring desires. Blocks can come in all sorts of forms from unexpressed emotions, muscle tension, a lack of inner peace or mental chatter.

Remember, you are an emotional, physical, intellectual and spiritual being so blocks will be encountered at all of those levels. Your assignment for the rest of life is to always be in conscious awareness to what could be blocking the natural flow of energy that connects you to all cosmic power. You are one with the Universe and it is essential that you honour that connection by releasing anything that will cause a disconnection to the flow of energy. The Universe is geared up to give you all you desire. You need to be available to receive it.

Have a think about what could be blocking you. Here are some ideas:

- Do you need to have a clearing conversation with someone? Are you ruminating over an issue you have with somebody and is that taking up mental bandwidth and causing negative chatter in your head?

- Do you need to de-clutter your home? If you desire new outfits then throw out or donate anything in your wardrobe that you no longer need. If your house is a mess with piles of filing and heaps of washing and unopened mail it is blocking your home from receiving in clean, fresh and vibrant energy. You exist in this space so this blocked energy is blocking you too.

- Do you need to have a massage? Tight and knotted muscles block your physical self from receiving in healthy, soft, light energy.

- Do you need to forgive yourself? Holding onto regrets, being bullish and demanding of yourself, beating yourself up all causes a mental block. Forgive yourself for being anything less than loving towards yourself and start afresh from today.

- Do you need to let go of control? Are you always pushing for an outcome or are you aware that you have a tendency to try to control people or situations? This is a very constricting energy. Why not set the intention to let it be? Let go and allow your energy to flow free.

- Are you angry? Do you need to bash a pillow, scream in the car while driving or write an angry letter and then burn it? As you know, anger is valid. It is also a powerful energy that requires transformation to ensure it isn't blocking you to love.

- Are you feeling connected to your Spirit? What do you need to do to foster that relationship with yourself? Do you need to journal? Perhaps take a walk or go for a run or have a candle-lit bath? You know what works for you.

- Is your mind cluttered with to-do lists? Why not get it all down on paper and unblock that poor brain of yours! Release and ease your mind.

ASK!

As we move into the next chapter on Manifesting, I would like you to get into the habit of asking for what you want. Asking is the first step to manifesting so let's get some practice in!

Start asking for what you want. Here are some ideas:

- Get into the habit of asking for help when you need it. Don't be a martyr!

- If your order in a restaurant isn't quite right, let the waiter know. Don't eat a plate full of resentment because you didn't speak up.

- If you are travelling economy but desire to be in business class, ask for an upgrade. Why not?! It's worth a shot.

- If you always wish your husband would open doors for you, let him know. Allow yourself to sit comfortably in your feminine energy and empower him to be in his masculine energy. Don't demand. Just let him know that you would feel cherished if he did that for you. Being in your feminine power is a beautiful energy for receiving.

- Ask for a discount! Again, you never know your luck! (I urge you to do this from a place of abundance and not lack. You are not being cheap. You know the Universe is abundant. This is simply a gentle exercise in practising the art of asking for what you desire.)

ASSESS YOUR DESIRES

Take a look at the following life areas again and consider what you desire in each:

physical health / fitness

money / finance

relationships with family / friends / colleagues

relationship with partner

career / work

spirituality / religion

adventure

learning

contribution

feelings / emotions

Consider what you desire today? This month? The next 90 days? The next year?

Once you have written your list of desires, journal about how you will feel once you have received them. I really want you to hook into the feeling of having everything you could ever dream of. The energy of emotion is so powerful and it is key to manifestation. I want you to prepare yourself on every level - physically, emotionally, intellectually and spiritually - to know in advance how your life will look and how you will feel when you have achieved all of your desires. When you know it in your being as if it has already happened, it is yours. You can't help but attract it in!

PUMP UP THE VOLUME

"New Shoes" - Paolo Nutini

"Live Louder" - Nathaniel

"Suddenly I See" - KT Tunstall

Mighty Manifesting!

"If your mind carries a heavy burden of past, you will experience more of the same. The past perpetuates itself through lack of presence. The quality of your consciousness at this moment is what shapes the future." Eckharte Tolle

I am so excited for you to have reached this part of the book! This is where you get to create your life and the really exciting thing is that it isn't hard. Truly! You have done so much work to connect you to the truth of you and you know that you are a spiritual being who is totally supported by a loving Universe. With that knowledge and having experienced that truth, manifesting is easy.

As a spiritual being you are a creator and so manifesting is your very nature. You are designed to do it with effortless ease. Indeed you have been manifesting your entire life! Almost everything that is happening in your life now is a direct reflection of all the thoughts, words and actions you have taken up to this very point. From now onwards your choice is to be a masterful manifestor and that means being conscious to your thoughts, words and actions.

As you read on I encourage you to hook into the power and truth of your Spirit. Read this from that place of truth rather than have your intellect try to 'work it out' and your ego try to belittle it. Open your heart and still your mind. This information is meant for you and it will be music to your soul!

In the chapter entitled 'Your Conscious Dream', you wrote about your vision as a tool to keep you focussed on your end goal when things felt tough. In the previous chapter you got clarity on your Daring Desires, taking into account your values and all that you have come to learn about yourself. Now it's time to refine that vision even more and make it happen.

But first, let's get you prepared to step into your mighty manifesting boots. You are a powerful being and I want you plugged into the mains to ensure you get to experience the absolute fullness of your desired life!

As you now know, you are an energetic being of pure love. Everything in this Universe is vibrating energy. Nothing ever stands still and everything is connected. You are a part of this energy. In the same way that one grain of sand on the beach is a part of the beach - there would be no beach without all the grains of sand - you are a part of the Universe. There is no separateness except the density and speed at which the energetic particles vibrate. The only difference between me and the chair I am sitting on is the vibrational speed and density of our particles.

Ok, so that's a seriously condensed snapshot of what energy is and how we relate to the Universe! For the purposes of this book I think that will suffice but I do encourage you to research more on Quantum Theory if this is of interest to you and I highly recommend Mike Dooley's books. Please know, however, that you do not need a degree in metaphysics to be able to manifest the life you desire!

We human beings are big bundles of energy and we each vibrate at various frequencies. When we feel sad or flat our frequency is low. When we feel bright and bubbly our frequency is high. You can literally feel that in your body. If you take a moment now to consider a sad memory and sit with that feeling for a few moments, I bet you will feel your state shift to match that vibration? You will likely feel low, grey and droopy. Then do the opposite. Think of something that makes you feel really happy or excited and feel how your vibration shifts. You will likely feel lifted, open and bright.

Vibrational frequencies are attracted to the same frequency. In other words - and I know you have heard this before - like attracts like. So it is usually the case that people on the same energetic frequency are attracted to each other. People who are victims to their conditioning, stuck in their stories and generally pessimistic tend to spend time around others who are also victims to life - they corroborate each other's opinions and thoughts and share in each other's woe. People who are determined to live a big and fulfilled life, who are committed to creating the best version of themselves every day and are generally excited and optimistic will spend time with like-minded people.

I bet you have heard it said that we are the sum of the people we mostly choose to spend our time with? It's so true! Take a look at the people you spend most of your time with and what does that say about you? I know I used to spend time with people who were victims of life because I was a victim too. When I woke up, chose to live consciously and love myself I was naturally attracted to people who had the same lust for life as me - and them to me.

If everything is energy then it figures that thoughts and beliefs are energy too. And, if like attracts like, then that gives our thoughts and beliefs tremendous power! You literally get what you think about and being careful of what you wish for is suddenly no longer a joke!

You can see what someone is going to manifest in their life by looking at their points of view. If you think life is hard, guess what you will create! If you believe life is easy and full of love, that is what you will get.

Your vibrational frequency is crucial to attracting all that you desire into your life.

When you are on a low vibration, your thoughts drop effortlessly into a pessimistic, victim mindset which attracts more of the same. Fear and shame are the lowest vibration.

When you are on a high vibration, it's easier to control your mind and choose thoughts that will serve you and bring you what you desire. Love is the highest vibration!

The secret is to align yourself to the frequency of your desires. When they originate from your True Self it is highly likely all that you desire is high-vibrational stuff because your authentic self is pure love and seeks only to attract equally high vibe goodness into your life. So whether you desire a fulfilling career, a loving life partner, a beautiful new car, an abundant bank account, joyful friendships - these sorts of things vibrate off the Richter Scale, not least because the experience of them make you feel great! Your assignment is to match your energy field to these desires.

The key to manifestation is intentionally choosing what you think about and what you say. Having control over your thoughts and your words is a muscle to be strengthened because for many, many years you have lived unconsciously, in reaction to your thoughts and without giving thought to the power of your spoken word. You have now chosen to live consciously and that means you get to create your thoughts, carefully choose your words and respond to life accordingly.

Mastery over your mind is so much easier when you are operating on a high vibration because you have the energetic capacity to work that mental muscle. In the early days of mastering your mind, it really can take some real effort on your behalf and I promise you it will get easier and more effortless. You will be greatly aided by feeling good - that will give you the energy to make the conscious effort to align your thoughts with how you desire to experience life.

So, before we look at what you are thinking and how that links to manifesting your desires, let's ensure you know how to keep that gorgeous vibration of yours raised. By the way, this is fun stuff. Raising your vibration means learning how to make yourself feel good and from this moment onwards, your biggest responsibility to yourself is simply to feel fabulous!

There are many ways to raise your vibration so I will share my top three favourites! This list will get you thinking and then you can add your own ideas. Remember, the key is to feel good!

Fun, Joy and Play - you need to play, laugh and have fun just as much as you need food and air and water! This is a chance to let your inner child free!

Children are pure spirits of love and they are driven to be on a high vibration. It is not in their nature to understand fear, lack, shame or anxiety. All of that is taught! They are ruled by their Spirit and all they want is to attract joy, love, ease and fun - so let's take a leaf out of their book.

Having fun doesn't need to cost a penny and can be as simple as having sex, dancing, trampolining, swimming in the sea, bike riding or playing with your kids.

I have fun and experience real joy when I am travelling, skiing, hiking, eating in great restaurants, hanging out with high vibe mates, doing yoga and dancing in the kitchen with my son!

You have just become clear on your values and desires so it should be pretty simple for you to choose a few things you could do to inject some fun into every day of your life. Why not commit to one thing every single day for the next 30 days and see what happens? I bet you will feel your vibration rise enormously!

I know that whenever I have honoured my desires around fun and play, manifesting has been so much easier. In fact, it has become rather effortless. Everything seems to just fall into place. So I make it a non-negotiable these days to inject fun, joy and play into my life. I admit, at first I found it hard to give myself permission to do this because there were always seemingly more important things to do or spend my time and money on. However, when I saw the impact that play had on bringing in my deepest desires, it seemed crazy not to be scheduling in fun!

Interestingly, in creating the new habit around prioritising fun, my desires have evolved to become more about creating joy and honouring desires that light me up so I have started travelling luxuriously, am learning to ski, enjoying the gym and being more present with my son. It's been a win-win!

I encourage you to do the same. Like any new behaviour it can feel clunky to start with but believe me when I tell you that creating joy in your life is just as important as breathing. Your vibration will thank you for it!

Gratitude - make a commitment to being grateful every day!

A shift into gratitude means you focus on all you have, no matter how big or small.

I think the most important lesson I have learned in the last few years is the power of gratitude. It's such a simple concept but oh so crucial.

At first I understood it on an intellectual level but as the years have passed by and as I get more and more in touch with my True Self and stay on my true path in daily conscious awareness, I 'feel' gratitude at ever deepening levels. It is quite astounding.

Sometimes I find tears running down my face for no reason other than complete humbling gratitude.

Even more amazing is that the more gratitude I feel, the more the Universe seems to support me. It just builds and builds and gets better and better. Sometimes I think I could burst with thanks!

This is an amazing concept for me because I used to be such a bloody victim! That was a terrible time in my life and a mindset that took some serious work to shift. Looking back, I can see how my victim mentality put me on such a low energetic vibration, often leaving me feeling fearful, sad or angry. A long way away from the love I so craved. I was trapped in a disastrous energy cycle which, at its peak, involved two house floods, severe anxiety, financial debt, depression and the company of people on the same path.

A victim tends not to see what they have in their life. Rather, the focus is on what they don't have and worse, what others have. That was me!

On the recommendation of my counsellor around that time, I listened to a Louise Hay meditation on gratitude in the desperate hope of shifting my life. In her meditation, Louise was thanking her fridge for keeping the food cold, her car for getting her from A to B, the electricity supply to her house and so on. That was my first introduction to gratitude and I thought she was a complete nutcase! I persisted with her bizarre meditations and it wasn't long before I too was grateful for all that we take for granted each day and I grew to love those meditations.

I am certain that practising gratitude saved my life.

Little by little my life improved and I slowly, slowly started to shift my focus naturally on all that I had and I started to feel rather rich.

For a long time my gratitudes were as simple as my beautiful son, a roof over my head, food on the table, loving friends and family.

Today my gratitudes are almost never-ending. I say them all day long!

Remember, where we place our focus is what we get more of. We attract what we think about. Being grateful means we attract more to be grateful for! So I encourage you to begin a daily practice of stating all you have to be grateful for.

Buy yourself a journal specifically for your gratitudes and commit to writing at least five things in it every day. A lovely practice is to write in your Gratitude Journal just before you go to sleep at night. It's a lovely high-vibrational energy from which to drift off into your dreams.

Affirmations – a tool to master your mind and your mouth!

At the end of every chapter in this book I have listed some affirmations so these are not new to you. However, I wanted to stress the importance of using them to strengthen your mind and support your manifestations.

If you get what you think about, then training your mind with positive affirmations that will serve you is key. Choosing thoughts that are positive will raise your vibration too. Affirming thoughts and a high vibration are key to manifesting so affirmations are going to become you new best friend!

Choosing to practise affirmations will also support you in developing healthy, conscious language. There is real power in our spoken word, not least because as the words leave our mouth it sends a strong energetic ripple throughout the Universe. When we say something it sends a signal to our mind that that is our truth - so it's important to watch your mouth!!

Your thoughts and words not only affect the outer experiences and results of your life, they also affect your physical health. Stressful, worrying and anxious thoughts mean our body is holding onto stress, worry and anxiety - all of which creates dis-ease.

"Every day in every way, I am getting better and better." Dr Emile Coue

Dr. Emile Coue practised medicine at the beginning of the last century and in addition to drugs, he would prescribe patients with the above affirmation to be said 20 times each morning and evening. He believed the way we think affects our health and felt that a combined mind and body approach was necessary to cure illness.

'I am getting better' has a much higher frequency than 'I am sick', wouldn't you agree?

Sure, you might be unwell but the truth probably is that you are slowly improving and you will be healthy again. Even if you are given a dire prognosis, there is plenty of evidence now to support the truth that you can heal your body by healing your mind; research has suggested that affirmations have a bio-chemical, neuro-chemical and neuro-pharmacological effect on the body. Telling yourself you are getting better will be of far greater service to manifesting health and recovery than reminding yourself and others regularly that you are not well.

If you notice that you have dropped into a low vibration such as fear, anger, worry or shame then you can use an affirmation to lift you into a higher vibration such as love, joy, trust, faith or hope.

The most powerful affirmations tend to start with 'I am' and there are many different ways you can begin your affirmation, such as I have, I love, I create, I enjoy, I allow, I invite and so on. The key is present tense, using words that imply abundance (so avoid using 'I want' or 'I need' or 'I must' because it implies lack), calm repetition and total belief in what you are saying, even if it feels a bit clunky to start with!

When you use an affirmation you are creating a new reality for yourself.

Here are some of my favourites:

I am love.

I am worthy.

I am safe.

I trust myself and I trust others.

I give and accept unconditional love.

I have an open and warm heart.

I live my truth.

I am grounded, present and connected to the power of the universe.

I am valuable.

I am significantly financially supported on a regular basis.

I am enough.

I allow fun, play and laughter into my life.

I am creating my reality.

I love to receive.

So go ahead and create your own affirmations. Notice the thoughts that are not serving you and choose a statement that will help you to create a new healthy belief. Stop lying to yourself and choose to tell yourself your own truths! You know yourself well enough now. What beliefs do you choose to live by? Notice how great it feels to recite those truths! You could record them into your smart phone and listen to them on repeat as you get ready for work; set them as alarms; write them on post-it notes and stick them about the house. You cannot see or hear these affirmations enough! Get them in your ears and in front of your face as much as possible and watch your life and the way you feel shift as a result. Your vibration is certain to increase!

Now that you have some ideas around how to keep that vibration of yours high, I would like to share with you my four steps to Mighty Manifesting!

1. YOU THOUGHT WHAT?!?

The first step to manifesting is to harness your mental power and take responsibility for your thoughts.

You are so powerful! You have proven your power by creating exactly what you have thought about for so many years.

If you struggle with creating wealth and you know that you have a belief like 'I have to work hard for money' or 'Money always disappears as soon as it arrives' or 'Rich people are greedy' or 'I can't be spiritual and have money' or any number of other limiting beliefs then that is what you will get.

If you struggle with intimate relationships and have a belief like 'Men are cheaters and can't be trusted' or 'I lose myself in relationships' or 'Marriage is boring', for example, then that is what you will create for yourself.

I would love you to take a moment and have a think (without judgement!) about what evidence you have to prove your power. What beliefs are you aware of that you can now see manifested in your life?

You have done so much work to uncover who you are, what you believe, value and desire, so hook into those truths and love yourself enough to up-level your thinking to that of a woman who knows her worth and understands the Universal laws that are supporting her every desire.

I invite you to get conscious to your thoughts and to notice when you drop into an old story or a fear-based belief or a copied pattern of behaviour. In that moment, choose to look within for your truth instead of being a puppet to previous generations. Cut the cord and ask yourself:

"How else could I perceive this situation?"

"What is the opportunity for my personal growth in this scenario?"

"What do I really believe about this?"

"How do I desire to respond to this?"

"What would be a loving way to interpret or respond to this?"

"I am willing to understand the love based lesson in this."

"I am angry but I am willing not to be and I choose to walk away, breathe and calm down before responding."

"I choose not to scare myself with that thought any longer and I choose to think X instead."

Remember, you chose this lifetime to learn lessons that would have you evolve to your next level. Your Spirit desired the experience of this earthly playground so your boundaries would be stretched and your buttons would be pushed and when you get conscious to your thoughts you can choose to dig deep within to understand why you are experiencing what you are. It is all your own creation and the purpose is all hooked into what you came here to learn, whether that be forgiveness, self-love, compassion, connection or any number of love-based lessons.

2. INVEST IN SOME NEW SPECS!

No, of course I don't mean that literally! But it is time to change your lenses and upgrade to something a little more rose-tinted.

The second step to manifesting is to get clarity on your vision. You've heard it said before but let me remind you: if you have been living unconsciously for a number of years then you will very likely be in the habit of thinking about what you don't have rather than what you do have or what you desire. Being a masterful manifestor means ditching the victim attitude and getting intimate with your desired vision.

When you think about something you subconsciously create a mental picture of that thing in your mind. Visioning is the same thing except you get to choose the picture. Your mind really doesn't know the difference between that image being real or imagined and it believes whatever you tell it, so far better to enjoy visioning a vibrant, fun healthy relationship, for example, rather than ruminating on whether he is trustworthy, who he is with, what he is doing etc. and torturing yourself with frightening images of betrayal. Why do that to yourself? Choose to switch channels – ask yourself what you desire instead and enjoy watching that movie on the screen of your mind.

There are many different ways to create your vision and the key is discovering what works for you. The most essential element to successful visioning is that you enjoy it! I will give you a few ideas but I encourage you to get creative and discover your own joyful way to create and enjoy your unique vision.

You can create a vision that is very specific – say, that new car you desire or the dream job or fulfilling relationship. You can also create a whole life vision if that takes your fancy. Literally anything goes. If a life vision freaks you out with overwhelm, just choose a couple of areas to focus on. Like I said, the key is that you enjoy the process. This is meant to be fun, not an onerous task!

When you are clear on what your vision is about, before you even start, I urge you to let go of any questions around how this is going to become your reality. Your vision does not include who you will call to make something happen or how the money will come in or which dating site the man might feature on! You have got to let go of the 'how' and focus on the result. Trust that the Universe will prompt you to take inspired action. For now, focus on the end game.

You can write your vision as a first person, present tense story. Maybe writing a wish list is more your thing. You could create a vision board of images that reflect your vision - either by cutting and pasting pictures onto a piece of card or pinning pics onto a virtual board online. You might like to read your vision into the recording device on your smartphone and listen to it as a bedtime story! Perhaps make your screensavers a collection of images that depict your vision. You get the idea - get creative!

Whatever method you choose, I encourage you to insert yourself into the vision and be specific about how you will feel while enjoying it. If you are writing a story, be sure to use sentences like, "It feels so great to be enjoying my loving family home" or, "I love the smell of the ocean air when I wake up in the morning" or, "Driving my car to work with the top down is so much fun and I love hearing the kids squeal with delight as the wind blows their hair about!" If you create a vision board, why not whack a few pics of yourself and perhaps your family throughout the board to illustrate that you are very much a part of all the elements. You could even add some words and affirmations to your board to give it a little extra oomph!

Although it's important to make your vision as clear as possible, I encourage you not to get really hooked on the minute details. Absolutely get specific about how you will feel but not so much around the details of the actual desire. The Universe will bring you the thing that will light you up and have you feel the way you desire to feel. You never know, you could even limit yourself by being too specific and if you get too hooked on details you could be blocking something better coming in! When I manifest I love to add a mantra to it along the lines of, "Thank you, Universe for bringing me my desires so easily. Thank you that they have exceeded my expectations!" - and I see myself laughing with joy that everything I desired arrived so quickly and effortlessly and was more than I could have ever imagined!

No matter how you create your vision, the idea is to engage with it every day for a few minutes. Spend some time looking at the picture board and connecting to how you feel to be a part of such an awesome vision. Sit with your eyes closed for 5 or 10 minutes and enter the vision that you wrote about. See yourself there and smiling! Feel it. Smell it. Taste it. And most importantly, enjoy it!

I like to write my vision as if I am describing a photograph - essentially I create a snapshot of my day. I get a little overwhelmed at the idea of sitting and visioning because I desire so much and I don't know where to start! So writing the snapshot first is really important for me. In my mind's eye I see that photograph and the details in it capture the key elements of a day in the life of me, living my dreams. I also like to write out my vision as a story and record it so I can listen to my own voice describing my perfect day. I get really animated and add lots of emotion and excitement to the recording so it feels totally real to me. I listen to it and just know it is my reality and that gets me excited! Sometimes I listen to it while working out - somehow moving my body at the same time pulls the vision into my body and I experience it at a deeper level. It's hard to explain but it works for me! I love vision boards too and I put pictures of my desires all over the place - on the wall, phone, computer, fridge! I also have a whiteboard in my kitchen which I have decided is magic!! I write things on it as a list and see it every time I make a cup of tea. It astounds me how quickly my desires come in when I write them on that board. My son has taken to adding his wish list to it too - he is already a mighty manifestor!

As much as it's imperative to hook into your vision every day, it's important that you enjoy that process, then let it go. You have a life to live today, don't forget, so don't allow yourself to miss the moment and escape to the future. That can cause anxiety and stress. Being present and loving the now is so important and it also means you can be alert to signs and signals that are guiding you towards your vision. The Universe will send you hints on the action you could take toward your desires so you need to be awake and aware, not lost in the future!

So go for it! Get creative and have fun!

3. AS IF!

Manifesting requires total faith and trust that your desire is a done deal.

The third step to manifesting is to take action and behave as if your desire is on its way. Because it is!

If you desire a new car and you believe you are going to have it, you need to behave in the way a woman would who is going to buy that car. You flick through magazines or jump on the internet and look for the car you desire. You might get a picture of it and stick it on your fridge to remind you of your imminent purchase. You can point it out to friends who pop over for coffee: 'Look! That's the car I intend to buy!' Then you would find at least a couple of car dealerships who stock your car and book in test drives (don't forget to take a selfie!). You would sit down with the sales person and talk finances. They would print you off a statement of costs, inclusions, finance options and so on. You would even start discussing what the best deal is they could do for you, because you are in conversation with another dealership. You get the idea!

You have to act AS IF.

You have to behave as if you are actually taking the steps required to have the thing you desire.

When you are taking these action steps, you get to FEEL what it's like to be that woman who has that thing. When you test drive the car, you get to smell the leather upholstery and feel the power behind the steering wheel and hear the awesome quality of the stereo! As your body is immersed in the experience it makes it all seem more real and you experience just how worthy you are of that car and how exciting it would be to drive it every day!

Hooking into the energy of how you will feel when your desire is your reality is key to manifesting it. It also feels really good to do that – and remember that feeling good means your vibration is raised, making you a magnet for your dreams.

I recently had an opportunity to go to Sydney for a business seminar and my desire was to fly Business Class for the first time. I had a lot to sort out to make this happen – I needed to carve out 2 weeks, put childcare in place, find the money for the entire trip and source a knock-out dress for the opening night party! The list was daunting, not least the funds to travel in style and luxury and my inner voice kept nagging, 'Economy class is still an option!' I am a Mighty Manifestor so I focused on my desire and I took action.

I booked the hotel in Sydney before I had the funds for the flight. I booked out the time in my diary and told everyone I was going and that I was excited to fly Business Class! I recited my wealth consciousness mantras every day and 'saw' myself boarding that plane and arriving refreshed and excited! Guess what happened!? Everything lined up beautifully. Even the dress! Some beautiful new business came in and voila, bring on the Aussie sunshine!

Lady, it is possible!

You are already doing it. You are already a Mighty Manifestor. The trick is to get conscious to your thoughts and actively guide them in the direction of your dreams.

4. LET IT GO! LET IT GO! (Yes, it's a 'Frozen' sing-a-long!)

I really want to encourage you to remember that the Universe is working overtime for you behind the scenes. Source energy desires that you have all you are meant for and there is a kaleidoscopic amount of energy shifting to line up your dreams. You have to trust this process in the same way that we trust that nature's intelligence will ensure that a flower will grow from the seed we bury in the soil. Germination is unseen but we trust the magic of creation is happening and at the perfect time, that first shoot will push through the earth.

I invite you to connect to the magic of creation. Choose to live in childlike wonderment and excitement for the revelation of your desires. It is coming. It is happening. It's on its way. Every time you doubt, the energy of that thought hinders and slows the miracle. So drop the drama and encourage the creation with joyful expectation of what is certainly about to arrive – and enjoy the process!

Experiencing the excitement of anticipation is all part of it. It's fun! It's an adventure! If everything was handed to you on a plate, life would be boring.

When you can't see any results, trust that the wheels are most certainly in motion and that every creation has any number of steps.

When you get a result that doesn't seem to be quite what you asked for, trust that your desire is still on its way and that you are still journeying towards the outcome. Allow the Universe to do her thing. She ain't finished yet and she knows how best to move you towards your desires in a way that has your highest will and good at heart.

Trust trust trust.

What you become in the process is a miracle to witness.

Knowing with total certainty that your desire is on its way allows you to take the pressure off yourself. The Universe has got this! You have done your part – setting your intention, getting clarity on your vision, mastering your thoughts and words, surrendering the outcome and taking action – and the Universe has heard you. There is no science to manifesting other than the basic rule that thoughts become things. There is no yardstick to perfection.

The truth honestly is that your best is good enough.

Be where you are at. You are not perfect and you never will be but with the intention and willingness to be a conscious, self-aware, loving, fulfilled woman, the Universe has seen you and has your back. So relax and be still in the knowledge that saying yes to yourself is enough.

Everything you have done to date as a consciously aware, Daring & Mighty woman is progress. You are moving in the right direction and in the same way that an aeroplane course corrects 90% of its journey, so too will you course correct when you notice you are off track because you are armed with the tools and knowledge to do so.

Be kind to yourself and commit to being lighthearted around manifesting your desires. I don't mean that you drop the fierceness around honouring your worthiness of them but I would love you to relax and let go of any worry and tension that will lower the vibration of your energy field.

Open up to receiving what is divinely yours and feel your energy expand.

Remember, your self-awareness means you know who you are and you have chosen to be guided by your True Self, which is enough, worthy, valuable, loving and loveable. You are compassionate and understanding and love yourself enough now to trust that you are always doing your best. Be free in that knowing and let the Universe work her magic!

Your vibration of self-love is magnetic. Miracles are coming your way with such ease and grace. All you need do is be available to receive your birthright!

I am so excited for you!

 *EXERCISES*

1. RAISE YOUR VIBRATION

1. Have Fun, Joy and Play - you need to play, laugh and have fun just as much as you need food and air and water. This is a chance to let your inner child free! Create time and make plans for including fun in your schedule! I encourage you to commit to one thing every single day for the next 30 days to get you started.

2. Practice Gratitude - make a commitment to being grateful every day! Start a gratitude journal and write at least five things in it every day.

3. Use Affirmations - a tool to master your mind and your mouth! As they come up, notice the beliefs and thoughts that are not serving you. Write each one down and then create an affirmation that is your chosen new belief to replace it.

2. MANIFEST

1. Take responsibility for your thoughts - consciously check in and choose thoughts that are your truth and that serve your vision.

2. Get crystal clear clarity on your vision - create and rehearse your vision in a way that lights you up and excites you.

3. Take action towards making your vision a reality - 'be' the woman who is living out your vision.

4. Surrender your vision - allow the Universe to do her thing knowing you have done your best and that it is enough.

3. DAYDREAM

This is a fun assignment to do when on a long commute or a during gym workout - the time will fly!

Think of one thing that you deeply desire. How do you feel when you think of this thing? When you have this thing, what can you see yourself doing? How are you behaving? Spend some time daydreaming about it. For example, if it's a new relationship that you desire, see yourself with the man and imagine what you would be doing, what conversations you would be having and how you would be feeling. Sit with the daydream and consistently go deeper into it. See it more clearly. Feel it more deeply. And then go deeper. Get even more clarity, using every sense. Feel yourself actually in the presence of this man and allow yourself to feel it to the degree that you are actually doing it.

Allow yourself around five minutes for this daydream. It doesn't need to take any longer and you can do it any time, any place. I love to get lost in daydreams when I am in the steam room and it's crazy how they start to become my reality!

4. VISUALISE

This isn't dissimilar to daydreaming, really. It also doesn't require more than 5-10 minutes of your time; however, I encourage you to commit to this every single day as a ritual. I would like you to set aside some time and space every day to sit and consciously intend your desires. Use that beautiful imagination of yours and enjoy the feeling of living out your desire.

Write your snapshot first so you have a clear image in your mind of what your vision is. If it helps you, record your voice reading the detailed snapshot of your vision so you can plug that into your ears while you visualise. Remember to turn up your emotional connection to the vision. Really feel yourself there and use your imagination to engage all your senses. By the end you should be bouncing off the walls with excitement for what is already yours!

5. MEDITATE

Meditation is a lovely tool to connect you to your source. As you meditate you become aware of your thoughts, bodily sensations and emotions. Every now and then you experience the bliss of nothing. No thought, no feeling. Just stillness and silence. Within that space of quiet is a glimpse of you as source energy - a part of all that is. It's hard to put into words because as much as this place is silent and empty, it is full of something so large I can't explain it. Suffice to say it's an awareness of your existence in a way that only your Spirit can comprehend and the peace that brings to the physical self is exhilarating. Experiencing this helps you to comprehend just how powerful you are because you glimpse the truth that you are absolutely part of the Universe and somewhere deep inside, you just know that manifesting your desires is your birthright.

Connecting with this truth means you will naturally start to manifest your desires from a place of empowerment. You know you are a creator.

I encourage you to meditate because it's a tool to connect you to the energy of the Universe and from that place, life seems to flow effortlessly. Manifesting can sometimes feel like a 'job' or something to be ticked off the 'to do' list but the truth is, a huge part of manifesting is about letting go. It's about surrendering to the Universe and allowing source energy to line everything up in the perfect way at the perfect time.

A lovely way to enter a meditation is to hold your attention on what you desire and then completely surrender it, spending the meditation in total detachment and enjoying a connection with the Universe.

Of course action is required to manifest your desires but it's important to keep hold of your stillness and peace. I encourage you to practise meditation as often as possible. Perhaps join a meditation group to support you. There are so many different styles and techniques taught so get out there and discover what feels good for you.

PUMP UP THE VOLUME

"Bhajan Speaks" - DaVinci, Erin Breech

"Grateful" - Rita Ora

"No More Drama" - Mary J Blige, P.Diddy

"Feeling Good" - Nina Simone

"Shine Ya Light" - Rita Ora

"Girl On Fire" - Alicia Keys, Nicki Minaj

"Girls Just Wanna Have Fun" - Cyndi Lauper

"I Can See Clearly Now" - Jimmy Cliff

"Let It Go" - Idina Menzel

"Make Believer" - Morcheeba

We Have Only Just Begun!

"Miracles honour you because you are lovable. They dispel illusions about yourself and perceive the light in you. They thus atone for your errors by freeing you from your nightmares. By releasing your mind from the imprisonment of your illusions, they restore your sanity."

A Course In Miracles

I am so proud of you!

You truly have proven yourself to be a Daring & Mighty Super Hero.

You have journeyed deep to discover the light that is you and now you get to shine that light on the world.

As a woman who has chosen to be masterful in all areas of her life, to love all parts of herself and honour her deepest desires, you are now a shining light that will inspire others to follow your lead, if that is their will.

Your personal transformation will have a far reaching impact on the rest of the world.

I hope you feel proud of yourself because it is only the rare few that dare to stretch beyond their sleepy comfort zone and awaken to what is possible for them.

Lady, you have done it and even more miracles await you.

Your assignment now is to love yourself even more fiercely than ever before. You have learned a brand new way to do life and that will take continued commitment, practice and persistence. So please be kind to yourself as you learn to walk again - this time in your truth, your power and with love.

In the same way that you continue to go to the gym to keep fit and keep your physical muscles strong, you are now being called to maintain a healthy relationship with yourself to keep your spiritual muscles fit and strong and able to support you, no matter what life throws in your path.

You are armed with so many tools and techniques to support you on your continued journey and I would like to draw your attention to my top three favourites that will keep you on track as you venture out into the world as a Daring & Mighty crusader.

1. CREATE AN ONGOING SUPPORT PLAN

As a warrior of self-love, I urge you to keep researching this subject. Don't just listen to me. I am not a one-stop-shop or a guru or master. There are others out there with different perspectives, ideas and life experiences. In the pursuit of being the best version of yourself, give yourself permission to insatiably indulge in your personal transformation. Enjoy *proving* the truth that you are loving, loved and loveable!

At this delicate time, it's more important than ever to consciously choose who you spend time with. As much as possible please do ensure the people you mostly hang out with are high vibrational and supportive of your journey and your vision. Being with people who know you are on a steep learning curve and who are available to support and encourage your change is key.

Remember to ask for help when you need it and be sure to ask it of people who are compassionate, understanding and excited about your process.

Align yourself with groups of people who are passionate about personal mastery and being the best they can be. Share stories of empowerment! There is something very powerful about a group dynamic that enables each individual to transform in a deeper, stronger way because of the power of joined minds. You may like to join my private Facebook Group – The Self-Love Hubb – to experience the power of masterminding. Here's the link: www.facebook.com/groups/theselflovehubb

In the same vein, please mindfully choose what you watch, listen to and read – keep it high vibrational, inspirational, motivational and joyful! Don't forget to subscribe to my free Spotify music playlist – The Self-Love Affair – to keep your vibration high! Here's the link: http://spoti.fi/1H0Gvz0

2. WRITE AS MUCH AS YOU CAN

Your journal is your new best friend. As important as it is to talk to your friends and mastermind with other truth seekers on the same journey, no one wants to be your journal! That's exhausting.

I have three journals and I use them to stay in connection with my inner wisdom:

1. Gratitudes – writing at least five gratitudes every day is a game changer. Remember, you get what you focus on.

2. Success and Miracles – witness and celebrate every baby step forward and every mini-miracle. Documenting your growth and the support of the Universe will mean you have proof that all is well when ego, fear and doubt knock on your door.

3. Expression, Clarity and Connection – dump your thoughts and feelings onto paper as often as possible. Create new awareness and express your feelings. Clear out anything that is blocking you to your truth and dig through the noise so that you may connect with the voice of your Spirit.

3. COMMIT TO A SPIRITUAL PRACTICE

At this sensitive time, it's so important to make time for your Spirit.

A spiritual practice means simply spending time with you.

Like any relationship, your relationship with yourself requires time, attention and energy. You have heard it said before – do what lights you up. Honour your Spirit and nurture that relationship by choosing regular activities and practices that have you feeling connected to you.

When you wake up each morning, ask yourself, 'How can I love myself today?' Then listen for the answer. You get to choose how you do your day and you get to do it with love, in conscious awareness and self-mastery.

Essentially, you will be starting your day by setting an intention. Consciously choose how you desire to feel and how you desire to interact with the world around you. Hand over control to your Spirit, knowing that she always operates with your highest will and good at heart.

You might like to vision and journal every day, meditate every other day, take a walk once a week, enjoy hot candle-lit baths three times a week, paint on Saturdays and enjoy tea, toast and magazines on Sundays!

When your self-love muscle is strong, it will be second nature to include spiritual practices into your day-to-day routine. In fact, life will feel off kilter and lifeless without them! In these early days it will probably help you enormously to diarise these practices into your schedule. If you value it, create time for it!

I encourage you to flip back through the pages of this book and reflect on all you have learned.

Look through your journals and remember your experience of each chapter. Then make your own notes on what you choose to embrace as new ways of living your life. What promises will you make to yourself? What vows do you intend to honour? What tools and techniques worked best for you and how will you commit to incorporating those into your life? Could you diarise specific times of the day and days of the week to spend time in spiritual connection? How will you commit to expressing your feelings as they come up? Who is in your Daring & Mighty tribe? You get the drift.

Personal responsibility is key now. It's up to you to maintain your change and create deeper transformation. This is a life-long process and you can choose to begin learning your lessons in a more joyful way from this moment on.

Here are some nuggets I would love you to take away from this book and I encourage you to add your own to this list.

- You are a beautiful Spirit - perfect in every way - and you are meant to be here.

- When in doubt, hook back into your 'Reason Why' - allow that to remind you why you chose to wake up and live consciously.

- Remember that fear is a story! Choose new stories that serve you.

- Dissatisfaction is a message from your Spirit, telling you it's time to grow.

- You are not your parents.

- You have the power to unlearn ways of being that are not your truth.

- Practise forgiveness - remember it's only you that hurts when you dwell on resentments.

- Your Spirit desires to be in the driving seat of your life.

- Give your mind a rest and *feel* your way to the other side of your problems.

- Take responsibility for your life - no one but you can create the change you desire.

- Depression is long term repression - safely express your emotions as often as possible.

- Journal, self-reflect and create new awareness - you can never know yourself too deeply.

- Regularly check in with all areas of your life - awareness is the first step towards change.

- Open your heart - compassion and forgiveness reside there.

- Challenges are an opportunity for growth - your Spirit desires to expand.

- Nurture your inner child - re-parent yourself and offer your little girl plenty of unconditional love, attention and understanding.

- Lean on your Spirit Team - The Universe, your Guides and Angels are all waiting to support you.

- Pray for miracles - they are your divine right.

- Self-love means loving all parts of you - your beautiful mind, your wondrous body, your delightful inner child and your spectacular Spirit.

- Commit to ways of loving all parts of you every single day.

- Hug yourself and say 'I love you!' into the mirror as often as possible.

- Make an act of self-care your daily non-negotiable.

- Be patient with your process.

- Your body is your headquarters - it's not who you are.

- Talk to yourself as if you are your own best friend.

- Stick your values on the fridge and commit to honouring those when a decision is required.

- Listen to your Spirit for your answers.

- Make loving choices.

- Live by your own rules.

- Mind your own business.

- Practise random acts of kindness.

- Have clearing conversations.

- Remember that how you feel is crucial to manifesting the life of your dreams.

- Give yourself permission to have fun, play and joy.

- Keep your vibration high - you attract where you are at.

- Use affirmations as a tool to master your mind and your mouth.

- Praise yourself often.

- Practise gratitude daily.

- Witness your achievements and congratulate yourself regularly.

- Honour your deepest desires - they are the voice of your Spirit and are meant for you.

- Decide to thrive.

- Meditate.

- Be available to receive.

- Ask for help.

- Remember that you are a creator and you get to design your life.

- Live 'as if'.

- Remember that your best is good enough.

- Relax, rest and be – develop the capacity to be still.

- Choose uplifting, nurturing, supportive thoughts.

- Rehearse your vision – keep it alive, fresh and exciting.

- Take action towards your desires.

- Surrender all outcomes to Universal intelligence.

- When you love yourself you do not need your partner or anything external to fulfil you – you are already full.

- Live the truth of your heart.

- You are the guardian of your soul.

- Be kind, compassionate, forgiving and understanding – to yourself and others.

- We are all here to learn how to love.

- We are all connected.

- Everything is love!

Lady, you are so beautiful, so valuable and so loved.

You know who you are and it is your time to shine.

The world awaits the humble and awesome glory that is your Spirit.

Trust yourself now and go and BE that woman you were put on this stunning planet to be.

I am beyond excited for you!

All my love,
Katie xx

 *PUMP UP THE VOLUME*

"Walking On Sunshine" - Katrina & The Waves

"Happy" - Pharrell Williams

"Pocketful of Sunshine" - Natasha Bedingfield

"One Day Like This" - Elbow

ABOUT THE AUTHOR

Katie Phillips is a Self-Love mentor and speaker who helps women to begin their Self-Love Affair so that they may live a Daring & Mighty life.

Katie mentors, coaches and teaches from a place of having really 'been there' and transformed her own life. She says, "Despite outwardly having a successful and exciting life, anxiety was 'normal' for me and I felt a sense of disconnection – like I didn't really know who I was or my place in the world. I made a decision to have a better life; a life that was a true reflection of 'me'. I could remain a 'victim' or I could choose to do something about it. So I did."

Katie believes that the key to success is an intimate relationship with your True Self. Her mission is to show women they can create a life they love by loving themselves first and she does this through private mentorship, luxurious private retreats, transformational group and online programmes.

Katie has a lifetime interest in spiritual and personal development. She is certified by INLPTA, with an NLP Diploma. She is a Reiki 2 Practitioner and a Graduate of the Hoffman Institute, the 'Advanced Transformation Academy' and the 'Gina DeVee Divine Living Coaching Academy'.

She is also an intrepid traveller, devoted mum, lover of Aussie wine and unapologetic day-spa addict!

Katie has been featured in many publications, including The Hoffman Institute magazine, Soul & Spirit magazine, Kids Health & Wellbeing magazine, Om Yoga, Hello!, Sussex Society magazine and on Positive TV.

To find out more about Katie visit her website: www.daringandmighty.com - and don't forget to download her free meditations from http://daringandmighty.com/meditation-library! You can also access 'The Self-Love Affair' music playlist on Spotify: http://spoti.fi/1H0Gvz0. You may also like to join her private Facebook group - the Self-Love Hubb - to experience the power of masterminding: www.facebook.com/groups/theselflovehubb

KIND WORDS

'As a true model of triumph and positivity, Katie Phillips paves the way for modern day women to know their worth, claim their value and radiate self-love. In an era that is awakening to the power of self-love, you'll find a mentor, a friend and hope in Katie and her book.'

Gina DeVee – International Success Coach

'Katie Phillips is an inspirational woman with the gift of bringing out the best in others, by helping them to see the best within themselves. If you want to be the greatest expression of yourself, then I dare you to have a Self-Love Affair.'

Sandy C. Newbigging - Bestselling Author

'Katie is a woman who writes from a life she has fully explored. Her heart is one she has allowed to open to life's joys and sorrows. Her words will inspire many others to live with adventure and drop their fear.'

Tim Laurence - co-founder of Hoffman UK and Bestselling Author

'Katie's book will help you move beyond self-limiting boundaries painlessly, to re-discover what existed all along - the love, power and pure magnificence that's really you!'

Stephanie J. King - Author of 'Divine Guidance'.

'This is a book of our time and without a doubt, this is an effective manual for women who are ready to roll up their sleeves and start loving themselves like their life depended on it. Katie shares her experiences, insight and deep wisdom in a heartfelt and conversational way, which makes this book highly relatable and difficult to put down! The exercises are practical but equally powerful and anyone who commits to working with this material will undoubtedly transform their lives for the better.

This book is a must-read for every woman!'

Desiree Marie-Leedo - Author of 'Invisible Goddess'

'Katie Phillips shares her wisdom in a down-to-earth, compassionate and humorous way. She guides you through the exact steps you need to take to achieve positive transformation in your life. This isn't just another transformational book. It's the ONLY transformational book you're ever likely to need.'

Stephanie J Hale - Bestselling Author

Made in the USA
Monee, IL
21 December 2021

86788351R00128